THE COLLECTIVE LEADERSHIP STORYBOOK
WEAVING STRONG COMMUNITIES

Karma Ruder
Lead Editor

Published by The Center for Ethical Leadership
1401 E. Jefferson St., Ste. 505
Seattle, WA 98122

Karma Ruder, lead editor
Design by SD33/Art Direction & Design

To order copies visit: www.ethicalleadership.org

Library of Congress Cataloging-in-Publication Data:
    The collective leadership storybook : weaving strong communities / W.K. Kellogg
    Foundation and the Center for Ethical Leadership / Karma Ruder, lead editor
    p. cm.

T 15328

ISBN: 978-0-975-5440-2-0

First Printing, October 2010

Printed in the United States of America on recycled content.

CONTENTS

ACKNOWLEDGMENTS

IN THE CREATION OF THE BOOK

Thanks go to the editorial weaving team—we have held the idea of this book for so long—and to the authors, poets, and other contributors whose insights and experiences made this book possible. Their names appear in the Contributors section at the end of the book. Their hearts and handiwork fill these pages.

Thanks go to Cheryl Fields who, in addition to being part of the editorial team, was responsible for coordinating the production elements of this book including proofreading, design, layout, and printing. She has worked with all of the graphics and pictures to make sure that the visual presentation of this work would illuminate the content.

Thanks to Myrna Schlegel who, as assistant editor, lovingly supported the creation of this book by relentlessly asking questions, editing, making suggestions, and re-editing so that this book would be clear and accessible as we strove to share the hearts as well as the lessons of the many writers. Thanks also go to Melissa Hamasaki and Steve Stapleton who read very many drafts and commented on them with grace, insight, and patience. Thanks to Anneliese M. Bruner for such thoughtful and careful proofreading.

FOR SUPPORTING THE WORK OF COLLECTIVE LEADERSHIP FOR COMMUNITY CHANGE

Thanks to the W.K. Kellogg Foundation for their long-term commitment to the belief that it is community wisdom that must guide community change. The Foundation has been on the pioneering edge of exploring how collective leadership can help reshape our institutions and systems to meet the challenges of the 21st century. They began this work as a bold experiment, and their continued partnering with communities has enabled us to all learn together. We thank them here because without their support, the stories told in this book would not have happened.

One of the toughest challenges of this book has been picking which stories to tell. We have been inspired and humbled by the work of the hundreds of participants who live collective leadership. They have given new meaning to and have taught us about deep hospitality, resilience, dedication to community, and laughter and joy in the face of the most challenging circumstances. There is no way to name all these people, and so we simply wish to thank them.

Finally, thanks to all the national team members who are noted in "A Story Behind the Stories." Their sharing of their talents, combined with their openness to learning from the participating communities, helped give shape to the work that these stories capture.

Karma Ruder
Lead Editor

Courtesy of the artist, Dr. Shelly Valdez

HOW STORY BEGAN

We Begin at the Beginning . . .

In the long ago time, Creator gave many gifts to the People: light, food, water, shelter. But Creator saw there was no order. The People would just run around waving their arms, pointing, bumping into each other. And Creator was puzzled by this behavior, and spent much time thinking about how to get the People to understand. And then Creator realized how quiet it was, and so Creator gave them sound and voice and the People hummed and shouted, but it was unintelligible. So Creator gave them words, and the People shouted and sang, but their revelry made no sense, just words heaped on each other with no order. So Creator gave the People language, a structure for the sounds and words, and the People spoke and they told each other what to do and used their words to build and farm and sing and dance and offer blessings and thanks for all the great bounty Creator had bestowed upon them. And slowly, they began to share with each other things that happened to them during the day and scary things they heard in the night. And slowly they began to pass on news to each other and use the gifts from Creator to tell each other how they came to be. And slowly the People passed on everything they knew to their children, so they could learn and grow and be strong and healthy. And the People called these tellings "Story." And Creator thought, this is good.

And so it was.

An original story by Lee Francis IV based on a Pueblo of Laguna tale.

INTRODUCTION

"And the People called these tellings Story." This story of where "Story" comes from was shared during a gathering in New Mexico and comes from the Laguna People. With its celebration of how important story is to being human, it is a perfect beginning to our book, which offers many stories about communities learning new ways to approach change. The people sharing these stories are eager to tell of their communities' experiences with a different kind of leadership that is springing up across the country.

This leadership is collective; it relies on the strength of relationships and pushes toward inclusion and justice. It is proving to be an approach that people hunger for, because practicing collective leadership makes us feel alive and joyful, even as we take on tough challenges. It allows us to be fully human, sharing our sorrows and our laughter. It does this by inviting us to be part of something bigger than ourselves, by acting on the belief that each community has the wisdom it needs to make a better life. We tap into that wisdom by sharing our stories, by asking many questions of each other, and by listening openly to the answers. Listening in this deep way forces us to cross boundaries and to share power with people we might ordinarily keep at a distance, and we begin to feel connected in a way quite unlike any other experience.

As we connect with others, we begin to find talents within ourselves that we did not know existed. We begin to offer these talents as gifts to the community. From these connections come unexpected solutions. Collective leadership that is based on the wisdom of the community keeps us learning while deepening our connection to an ever-widening circle of people. It is in this way that we create a new story for our community.

While each story in this book is unique, all reflect a desire to weave a new social fabric, one that holds values of caring, mutuality, family, love, and accountability—in short, a social fabric woven with a high expectation of everyone doing their best for the common good.

To others also interested in weaving a new social fabric, this book offers ways of working together that make this possible. We have learned that there are patterns of working together that, when continually woven into our daily efforts to create community, bring forth a resilient, colorful and vibrant whole cloth. This social fabric is strong and keeps us warm and safe as it holds us all. These patterns of working together, enacted, create a way of life that we refer to in this book as *collective leadership*.

At the end of this introduction, we will come back to these patterns of collective leadership, giving a brief description of all of them. Each chapter will explore one of these patterns in detail, and will share the stories of people and their communities that are making the practice of collective leadership a way of life.

Between these chapters, we offer poems and other forms of story that capture the feelings of those doing this work of community weaving. There is also a final section offering resources to support the ideas you will find in this book.

But first,

HOW THIS BEGAN

This book tells stories of collective leadership efforts that have grown out of a program that began in 2002.

The W.K. Kellogg Foundation initiated a new leadership program based on a simple premise: If institutions and systems that serve communities are to be successful in meeting the needs of their members, then more people from all parts of the community must engage in reshaping those institutions. The Kellogg Leadership for Community Change (KLCC) program was launched to promote collective and culturally appropriate leadership in communities across the country, and marked the next progression in the Foundation's long history of leadership development programs. One guiding premise of KLCC was that in order for communities to build the capacity needed to make these changes, opportunities would need to be created for those often left out of decision-making processes to contribute and develop their own skills. From the beginning, the Kellogg Foundation, the communities, the partners and all those involved knew that unless we drew on all the community's wisdom and gifts, we would not find our way.

Sharing our gifts. Photo by Tony Lowe

This is one of those simple, but not easy, propositions. In many of our communities, people feel powerless and too isolated to believe that anything can change in a positive direction. Often, people who have great talents and gifts lack the confidence to see them and claim them because they have never had the loving support needed to test their own limits. Too often, well-meaning outsiders have gone into communities, seen this lack of confidence, and applied answers that worked somewhere else. Without a full understanding of the differences in local traditions and history, these answers are not likely to yield the intended results.

The challenges in our communities go beyond what we can accomplish with a one- or two-year project. Instead, we are striving to cultivate a way of life. This work connects those inside and outside of institutions in ways that allow everyone to bring her/his gifts, energy, and love of community into the work.

Using collective leadership challenges us to move beyond the traditional view that developing individuals to be "the leader" will solve the problems that we collectively face. Helping individuals to develop their gifts and to offer them in service of something they care about is still of critical importance, but it is not enough. More and more, groups and networks are seeing the need to learn new ways of sharing power and resources to advance common purpose.

One important network you will hear about throughout this book is a growing national community of organizations and individuals who are creating change in their communities through the practice of collective leadership. The Community Learning Exchange (CLE) grew out of the lessons of collective leadership. The CLE offers an opportunity for communities physically distant from each other to support and extend each other's efforts. More information about the CLE is included in our stories and in the Resources section at the end of the book.

WHAT DEFINES COLLECTIVE LEADERSHIP

Some condensed definitions of collective leadership from people doing the work in their communities include:

- the collective soul in action;
- people, power, and place;
- mobilizing collective spirit and wisdom into action;
- speaking truth, in love, to power; and
- relationships in action that advance justice by trusting shared wisdom and liberating individual gifts.

More specifically, collective leadership is a way for diverse groups of people in our communities to hold purpose, direction, and action cooperatively. It calls for us to build deep relationships with each other and to be willing to cross the boundaries that keep us from joining with those who share our purpose—whether they are boundaries of race, age, culture or history.

With the trust that grows from cultivating relationships comes a willingness to share power among people and organizations. As the group learns together, participants open to new ways of arriving at long-term goals.

Additionally, as already mentioned, collective leadership actively seeks to include those who previously have been left out of leadership positions. Those who traditionally have been marginalized hold wisdom that is essential to the success of the whole community.

The final hallmark of collective leadership as discussed in this book is that it starts with community. It is critical to know your community, its history and its heritage before you undertake change processes. We have learned that the answers the community is looking for will always come from the deep wisdom of those who know and love their particular place, and who are willing to dedicate their time and treasure to making it the best place possible.

As you can see, collective leadership requires us to expand our notion of leadership from the solo perspective of "I" to include the powerful "We"— keeping both the "I" and the "We" as equal partners.

Collective leadership offers the space for working through tensions created by past injustices, exclusion and alienation. It allows for the healing needed to move communities forward. It offers a hopeful way to move communities toward a healthier, more just, and more inclusive future.

WHAT COLLECTIVE LEADERSHIP IS *NOT*

We find that when people hear the term collective leadership, they often leap to some conclusions that are neither correct nor helpful. Since some groups have spent a fair amount of time working through these common misconceptions, we offer a few thoughts on what collective leadership is *not*.

- *Mistaken notion #1—Everyone works on everything together.* Instead, collective leadership means that once people have arrived at a sense of the whole undertaking, which does require everyone's time, then the work is done by those with the gifts and interest to move the work forward.

- *Mistaken notion #2—Everyone has equal say.* Instead, collective leadership means listening to those who want to contribute ideas and valuing their perspectives.

- *Mistaken notion #3—Collective leadership replaces individual development.* In fact, when collective leadership is in action, the group supports individuals to take risks, and to be open—a process that promotes individual development.

- *Mistaken notion #4—Collective leadership means making decisions by consensus.* While consensus can be used as a decision-making model for collective leadership, it is not the only way that decisions can be made. Often, some part of the group is more focused on a particular aspect of the work and is in the best position to make decisions. What is important is that all decisions include a sense of the whole group's intentions.

WHY THIS BOOK

This storybook is a practical yet inspirational companion piece to *The Collective Leadership Framework Workbook,* which is designed to guide communities in a step-by-step process to develop collective leadership. (Check the Resources section to find how to get a copy.) The premise of the Workbook is that when we are open to learning and willing to ask questions, we develop better solutions. This commitment to being open to learning is a core element of collective leadership and is inherent to the ways of working together that we will explore in this book.

When you invite people to use their creativity, there are many imaginative and successful ideas that emerge. Our intention is to show some of the many different ways that communities have lived the collective leadership that the Workbook outlines.

As you might expect, because collective leadership celebrates and thrives on diversity, the story of collective leadership needs many voices to tell it. Within this book, you will meet individuals from around the country sharing their communities' experiences with this way of changing community.

Additionally, there are five of us who have served as weavers, who have gathered this material together and speak on behalf of the many people who have been part of the formative stage of this work. In the spirit of this work's commitment to keeping the "I," even as we move into the powerful "We," you will find that each chapter reflects the author's unique vantage point, even as the chapter shares wisdom learned as a group. We hope our decision to respect the individual voices while sharing the community's wisdom will enrich your understanding of this material.

Although this is a how-to book of sorts, it is not one in the traditional sense. It is less about **what** to do and more about the importance of paying attention to **how** you do it. The stories in this book tell of a method of working with others that is based on ways of **being**. These ways of being have proven so rewarding that, for groups who have engaged in them, they have become a way of life.

In this book are insights into these ways—or patterns—of engaging each other that make people want to fully show up and to remain faithfully involved. Hearts full of love and laughter are more likely to stay with the work so that it can gain momentum and community change can be realized.

AND WHAT ARE THESE PATTERNS?

There are four patterns that, when practiced together, form collective leadership capable of weaving a new social fabric.

Pattern #1: We take time to form deep relationships with each other.

Chapter 1 focuses on the importance of forming deep relationships. Once we have built trust and connection, we can have the tough but essential conversations that move us through stuck places so that we can learn from one another and share power.

One process that supports this pattern of working together is Gracious Space. We use Gracious Space as a way to create a collective spirit focused on bringing our best selves to the work.

In this chapter, various storytellers share their experiences of being transformed by opening to relationship.

Pattern #2: We cross boundaries that keep us from working with others who share our purpose.

Chapter 2 explores what it means to cross boundaries that have kept groups or communities from working with those whose contributions could help move the work forward.

One process that supports crossing boundaries is peacemaking circles. The circle process starts with the idea that we are all whole, and we often need help remembering and acting on that truth.

In this chapter, we share a story that reminds us of the courage it takes to step into the history of our communities in order to heal past hurtful exchanges. There are also stories about crossing the boundaries of race, geography, and age as well as a story that invites us to ask who we see as belonging to our group.

Pattern #3: We trust community wisdom and tap into it to find the answers it holds.

Chapter 3 explores the third powerful way we work together in collective leadership—we look for the answers to our community's problems by trusting the wisdom of those who live in the community. This process calls for compassion, because we ask people to share what they think and feel.

Building trusting partnerships based on mutuality is a key process that supports this pattern. Mutuality can only exist when each participant acknowledges and benefits from the contributions of the other.

This chapter includes several short stories as well as an extensive case study about what happens when we act on trust in community.

Pattern #4: We know our story and together imagine the narrative for our community.

In Chapter 4, storytellers demonstrate how story helps us to discover who we are in a way that honors the past, frames the present and imagines the future.

The creative process of storytelling is critical to forming identity, analyzing data, creating strategies for change and opening up imagination and creativity. Storytelling cultivates personal, organizational, and community change through questions and conversation.

The storytellers in this chapter use their own stories to show how we can create new narratives for the future of our communities.

At the end of this book is a Resources section. Here you will find primers and additional information on the processes that enable collective leaders to engage in these patterns.

These patterns of working together allow people to become fully alive and joyful in their work. Yet they are not easy to carry out—especially in the beginning. This is because they are so different from the ways we are used to dealing with each other within most organizations and institutions. The act of unlearning those old habits in order to learn a different set of patterns of engaging each other, a different kind of leadership, is an act of love and commitment.

To do this work you must be ready to live at your learning edge and to confront the habits that keep you from being your best. We welcome you who believe it is time to live out our acts of love. This book is for you—to show you it is possible and how you can begin.

The Editorial Weaving Team
Karma Ruder, Center for Ethical Leadership
Dale Nienow, Center for Ethical Leadership
Francisco Guajardo, University of Texas, Pan American
Miguel Guajardo, Texas State University, San Marcos
Cheryl D. Fields, Langhum Mitchell Communications

A STORY BEHIND THE STORIES
Background to help you understand some terms in the stories

K LCC. You will find those letters on the lips of many storytellers in this book—always said with affection and gratitude. KLCC stands for Kellogg Leadership for Community Change. As mentioned in the introduction, the W. K. Kellogg Foundation started the initiative that has guided all the storytellers and their organizations in developing collective leadership.

Eleven organizations stepped up to do this work on behalf of their communities. This collective leadership experiment included two multiple-year sessions. In the first session, six sites focused their collective leadership efforts on improving the quality of teaching and learning. The five sites in the second session focused on youth and adult partnerships, and on how crossing the boundary of age could result in communities that are more just.

Each organization was asked to create a leadership team that included these roles: **project lead**—responsible for the overall work and for connecting the learning back to the organization; **coach**—responsible for skill development and for learning through doing the change work; and **evaluator**—responsible for inviting people to reflect, improve, and be responsible for capturing the learning as the work progressed. You will hear mention of the coaches and evaluators in these stories.

At the core of the work was a group of diverse individuals from these communities who became fellows. The **fellows** were community members and positional leaders who jumped into the experiment of learning how to practice and develop collective leadership. These people learned skills, defined the work they wanted to do and carried it out. You will hear of fellows and of fellowship in these stories.

The program also included an opportunity for the leadership teams and the fellows to come together during national meetings, called **national gatherings,** as well as to share at **Community Learning Exchanges.** These occasions to connect proved to be an essential part of the learning process. Not surprisingly, these events are mentioned frequently.

Additionally, a national team supported the work of the leadership team and fellows on behalf of the communities. One part of the national team, the **Coordinating Organization**, developed the **Framework** we discussed earlier, coached the coaches about how to use it and how to address local challenges, and created the national learning community to support peer learning. Other national team members focused on communication strategies and effective evaluation. Members of the national team are also responsible for this book.

The eleven organizations named below were the first to explore the collective leadership model described in this book. For those of us involved, the relationships continue regardless of the level of funding. One of the early questions everyone had was what would happen as the KLCC funding and support ended—would the work end? It did not. Collective leadership has a contagious quality to it and, instead of collective leadership efforts dwindling, its practice has spread to other groups who were never funding recipients.

Collective leadership, by its nature, is not something you do alone. Neither is it something that requires endless funding and technical support. As you read this book, you will find many ideas and processes that can get you started. Yes, it is time-consuming and hard work. It is also so transformative that it is likely to become the starting place for all your plans and actions.

THE FIRST ELEVEN
Throughout this book, you will see references to the following organizations:

KLCC Session One
Building Public Will and Action Towards Quality Teaching and Learning

The Public Policy and Education Fund of New York
(Citizen Action of New York)
Buffalo, New York

New Mexico Community Foundation
Pueblo of Laguna Department of Education
Eastern Cibola County, New Mexico

The Llano Grande Center for Research and Development
Edcouch-Elsa, Texas

Salish Kootenai College
Flathead Reservation, Montana

New Paradigm Partners Inc.
Northwestern Wisconsin

MIGIZI Communications, Inc.
Twin Cities, Minnesota

KLCC Session Two
Valuing and Building Youth-Adult Partnerships to Advance
Just Communities

Boys and Girls Club of Benton Harbor
Benton Harbor, Michigan

Big Creek People in Action
Caretta, West Virginia

Roca Inc.
Chelsea, Massachusetts

Mi Casa Resource Center
Denver, Colorado

Lummi CEDAR Project
Lummi Reservation, Washington

National Team
Coordinating Organization
Center for Ethical Leadership
Seattle, Washington

Institute for Educational Leadership
Washington, D.C.

Innovation Center for Community and Youth Development
Takoma Park, Maryland

Dorsey & Associates LLC
Sarasota, Florida

National Communications
Langhum Mitchell Communications
Washington, D.C.

National Evaluation Team
Headed by Maenette K. P. Ah Nee-Behnam,
University of Hawaii at Manoa, formerly of Michigan State University

FRIENDSHIP AND ART
by Ansel
AKA Hector Morales

Friendship is one thing that drives my character

in order to help the Community.

And remember this:

what we are doing is art.

And art is NEVER finished

It's only ABANDONED!

Photo by Juan Ozuna

CHAPTER ONE

RELATIONSHIP IS THE FOUNDATION FOR SUSTAINABLE CHANGE

by Karma Ruder
with Liji Hanny, Marsha Timpson, Mariah Friedlander,
Harry Goldman and Gayle de'Sousa Warner

What is it about collective leadership that draws us to it and makes us want to stay with the work over time?

In this chapter, we explore the first pattern of working together that collective leaders cultivate: **We take time to form deep relationships with each other,** *building trust and connection with each other, creating an environment of loving support.*

The richness of deep relationships brings color and vibrancy to the weaving of our social fabric. It offers us a sense of belonging and renewal.

Opening to relationship changes us. This chapter offers a number of stories from people around the country, along with Karma's thoughts about the lessons these stories hold. Our hope is that as you listen to so many different voices, you will sense how belonging and renewal emerge from this way of working together.

The Editors

Individuals get involved in community change work because they want to do something that will make a difference for people they care about, or help a community that has been important to them. We have learned in increasingly profound ways that relationship is at the core of sustainable change work. The process of developing collective leadership gives groups staying power over time. It does this by providing a way for diverse people who care about a common cause, even if they have argued or clashed in the past, to come together and to build trust and safety, step-by-step. With trust and safety comes commitment.

When we take the time to learn each other's stories, to identify each other's gifts, and even to accept the habits that we perceive as annoying, we make the time to fall in love with the work and with those committed to it. This respectful and joyful learning becomes a way we help each other move through the stuck places of old assumptions and old stories to a place of new possibilities and creativity.

People are hungry to be seen for who they are, and to be accepted as they are, gifts and challenges alike. When the work allows people to be who they are, they keep coming back to do the next phase, to take on the next challenge, to be in the work as a way of life—as a journey and not just a series of goals to be met.

In collective leadership, as the group supports and mentors individuals, the individuals grow stronger. In turn, as increasingly confident individuals take risks, the group becomes stronger and is more able to stand together in difficult times, more able to take action. Situations in which all parties thrive are, in fact, what most of us strive to find in our lives.

During one national gathering, we asked communities to define what "just communities" meant to them. The response from those working in the Lummi CEDAR Project was to share their concept of *Schelangen*, a Lummi term that speaks to the Lummi way of life and way of being. Their clear understanding—that justice emerges when people live according to deep principles of good relationship, good attitude, and good behavior—gave everyone listening a powerful moment of insight. It reflects why being in good and loving relationship with each other is at the heart of collective leadership and informs what we do and how we do it.

We have seen many instances of powerful change work that started with an individual or a group changing from the inside out. Former adversaries become respectful partners as they work towards common goals; a group shifts its plan to go where opportunity is open, to work with others who are ready to see that an institution or a system needs to try something different. It is easier to open to new situations when we feel safe. Feeling safe is one of the outcomes and benefits of the net of deep relationships we develop in collective leadership.

Being in deep relationship also changes how groups approach planning. Instead of starting with a detailed plan that is followed step-by-step until completed, a group becomes clear about its shared purpose and direction in the process of learning about each other. That process of learning about each other, so key to collective leadership, requires us to be present in the moment. When we are paying attention to what is going on now, we are able to respond to an opportunity as it emerges. Leadership based on relationships is shared and flexible leadership that welcomes learning and adapting as we move forward.

In this chapter, we share stories about what happens when we intentionally let go of old ways of relating, open ourselves to risks, and creatively engage with each other.

In a number of these stories, you will read about Gracious Space, a methodology we introduced to help people work together better. At its core, Gracious Space is about intentionally bringing our best selves to the work and challenging each other to stay open to new perspectives while learning in public. This process moves from the inside out. It asks people to consider their own contributions to whatever is happening and to be ready to let go of old habits and ways of thinking that get in the way of moving forward together. It invites people to see mistakes as opportunities to learn what will work better, and to adapt to unexpected developments.

We often say that you can learn the concept of Gracious Space in five minutes and it takes a lifetime to master BEING Gracious Space. In the Resources section at the end of the book, we have included the five-minute version with a few easy first steps and we tell you where to find more in-depth material. We hope the stories in this chapter, which share what happens when individuals and groups practice Gracious Space, will encourage you to pursue this powerful methodology.

Our first story comes from Liji Hanny, Director of Operations at the Boys and Girls Club of Benton Harbor. This story shows what it means to let go of old assumptions and answers and to truly open up to the gifts of others. As you will see, when people shift to this pattern of working together in which the importance of relationship shapes all they do, significant change and positive outcomes result.

....

SEEING THE GIFTS
by Liji Hanny

It used to be that at the Boys and Girls Club, we pushed young people out when they turned eighteen. Our focus was six-to-eighteen year olds and we didn't know what to do with young men and women as they turned older and didn't fit our model of youth development. We looked at young people as recipients of service, almost like a commodity. Now, we really see that each young person has a great gift to offer, something to teach the rest of us. It's just a matter of seeing it and finding the right place for them to give it.

Now, I hire those young people who have been in the program and learned how to give their gifts and take responsibility for contributing and helping others come along. Our staff is a lot younger than it used to be. Those young people know more about what the teens need and what they are talking about than any of us who are a lot older. We had to work together to get to that place where they could work through their issues and learn how to give their gifts.

A big turning point for us happened at our first national gathering of communities working on developing collective leadership. At that gathering (in Olive Branch, Mississippi), our group met other youth from all around the country and from very different cultures. One group, from the Lummi Nation, was especially different from us because their cultural heritage is based on youth listening to elders as a way to learn the culture. Their youth are much quieter than ours. Our group was 98 percent African American and in our culture we are jestful, we tease each other, we make light of problems as a way of dealing with them.

When our youth treated the Lummi in the same way we are accustomed to treating each other, that caused a lot of hurt to the Lummi youth. There were discussions about this at the national gathering and we continued them when we got home. At first, our youth said, "We

Liji Hanny (center) conferring with youth from the Boys & Girls Club of Benton Harbor at the KLCC National Gathering in Olive Branch, Mississippi. Photo by Isaac Singleton

didn't do anything. We were just joking." It took a second round of talks before our youth saw that they had, in fact, crossed a line. Our youth began to see how one little word in jest can really hurt another person, how thirty seconds of using the English language in a bad way can take a lifetime to fix.

At the gathering, our youth saw that others besides themselves had trials and tribulations, including the Lummi. Our youth went to Mississippi assuming everyone was just like them. Now, they can see that everyone is different. Our youth became great friends with the youth from Lummi. And once our youth could see that the Lummi were different, they could see that was true at Benton Harbor, too, and that the differences are what's cool.

At the gathering, we were introduced to Gracious Space as a way of listening with compassion. When we got home, we continued to use Gracious Space to figure out what respect really meant and what we expected from each other in this work. When we began to listen to each other with intention, and to go to some really deep places, that was a real turning point.

Not only did our relationship to the Lummi shift, but this new way of interacting changed how we related to each other in Benton Harbor, too. For example, we were at a meeting and one of the youth fellows, Nia, came late. No one knew why she was late, but everyone could see she was upset. Everyone wanted to know what was wrong. Finally, Nia raised her head and, with tears streaming down her face, said, "My dog died." "Your dog died! You're making a big deal over that?" someone asked and began to laugh. But then, one of the youth who had attended the gathering said, "Wait a minute. She loves her dog. Even if you don't care that much about your dog, she cares about hers. We need to respect that." And the room changed.

We still struggle with this—for thousands of years we have been programmed to take the air out of the room. People say, "I don't want to hear all that touchy-feely stuff." That is, until it's their problem.

As we began to move in this new direction, we also moved from being a program that mentors young people to one that partners with them. What we have learned is that it isn't what you do as much as who you are. You have to embrace change, take risks and make room for others to use their gifts. Everybody has a gift if you are willing to see them in that way instead of as somebody that needs what you have to give them. When we acted on what we learned, the numbers of youth coming here more than tripled and has stayed high.

Here are some examples of how our collective leadership work has spread out and touched other people and programs in Benton Harbor.

Our fellows picked education as their priority for their change work. One of the programs that they started was a tutoring program to help high school students. The youth fellows were very much involved in all the decisions about what we wanted to do with the tutoring, including hiring the tutors. So the tutors knew something about youth and adult partnerships coming in.

The tutors told us that there were better ways to offer tutoring than what we were doing, but we told them that we knew what we wanted. This last year, I realized that we were not honoring our partnership with the tutors. It was just like working with the youth. These tutors brought in gifts about knowing how to tutor that we weren't using. So this last year, when we brought them in to work with the youth in the main building, I told the tutors that we would give them a space and let them do whatever they wanted to do in it. At the end of the program, we had sixty young people who improved their reading by three grade levels. Now we know that this program is a keeper.

Another priority for our fellows was working with parents. We started doing workshops for parents to help them understand what they could do to help their sons and daughters do better in school and get to college. We have continued doing that. I am very proud that every one of our KLCC youth fellows graduated and went on to college—that is not the case for many of the students in our high school.

This work continues to spread to many other places in our community. Everyone who has touched this youth and adult partnership work has been transformed by it, and takes it into their own work. Our first coach is now working at the local college and is bringing in youth to be part of decision making there; that is new for the college.

Our evaluator is now a principal at a middle school and an interim principal at two others—and she is bringing all this learning into those schools. Our youth are confident and as they go on to college they are taking responsibility for their own lives, knowing that they have great gifts to give. At first, I was worried whether these changes would end when our youth fellows left for college. Now, James has trained Benino to do all the audio-visual work around digital storytelling that he learned, and Benino is carrying on those lessons. We have new young people stepping up to carry on the work. They don't know that we used to do things differently because now it's all just Boys and Girls Club and the way we do things.

THE PLACE WHERE WE LIVE

The Framework used to guide development of collective leadership (which you can find more about in the Resources section) stresses that collective leadership begins with knowing our community. When we understand the history and heritage of the place where we live, that knowledge cultivates deep roots to hold the change work. When we take the time to know and understand our stories of place, we understand each other better and understand what will work for us in our place, our community.

In this next story, written by Marsha Timpson, Learning Coordinator at Big Creek People in Action, we learn how a shared relationship with place can help people of different generations move into deeper relationships with each other.

Marsha models radical hospitality through her work with collective leadership. Her love of place and her ongoing commitment to service learning attracts many students who learn by giving their work and, in return, receive an education rich in the wisdom of community.

....

TAKE ME HOME COUNTRY ROADS
by Marsha Timpson

Twenty years ago a group of individuals came together with a goal to better the water quality of our community. They called themselves Big Creek People in Action (BCPIA) and didn't know then that they were beginning a long journey. They started with their dream of developing a better future for our community, and we have continued that dream and are now beginning a new phase in the journey to ensure a just community.

A few years ago, BCPIA was fortunate enough to be chosen to be a part of Kellogg's Leadership for Community Change Session II program. The focus of Session II would be to develop youth/adult partnerships to bring about community change. At BCPIA, I think we were a little smug about getting involved in this program because we *thought* we already knew all about working with youth. BCPIA had always had youth as an integral part of our organization. We had youth serving on our board of directors, we had a youth program called Young Leaders Action Council, and there were always young people in the building for one thing or another. We *thought* we would have all this wonderful funding from the Kellogg

Foundation to help us do what we were already doing—mentoring young people. Adults teaching the younger folk all the wisdom we had accrued over all the years!! We weren't quite sure where the "partnership" part came in, or why they chose to phrase it that way—but we **did** know that we already had a handle on this stuff and were old hands at it. Ha!!! Boy, were we old folks about to learn a lesson! It was a good lesson to learn—but definitely still a lesson.

The adult fellows began this project by trying to determine what things we wanted to impart to our youth, and what it was we needed to do to teach them and inspire them. We thought that this collective leadership program expected us to be the "teachers" and the young'uns to be the "students." That, of course, was never the intention. They had NOT made up a catchy phrase called youth and adult partnership, even though what they *really* meant was adults teaching youth. Nope, it was just our tunnel vision that thought that was the way it would be. We very quickly discovered the program was not going to follow that path. And we began to realize these young'uns were teaching us as much, or more, than we were teaching them. What did we know about computers, digital stuff, and all this new technology? Not much at all!!!! They, on the other hand, were absolute whizzes at it.

There were many of these lessons learned along our journey to this youth and adult partnership—the most important one being that it wasn't so much an issue of "teaching" as it was "sharing." We shared our knowledge with them and they did the same with us. The adults and youth became friends first and partners second. We knew we had a common goal of community change work that we wanted to accomplish, but we also just had fun together. Throughout our journey we put together floats for local parades, refurbished the pool house for our local swimming pool, volunteered at all the events that BCPIA sponsored and even had our own events, such as our annual Diversity Day Dinners.

Did we start out this way? Heck, no! When did I see us turn the page and begin to be a true youth and adult partnership? I think, for me, it was during the preparation for our "Country Roads" presentation at the national gathering of the communities developing collective leadership in Olive Branch, Mississippi. The fellowship, as a whole, was so terrified and intimidated at the prospect of this presentation. The only thing we completely, absolutely and wholeheartedly agreed upon about this presentation was the fact that we did not want to do it and that we were scared to death. We (youth and adults) felt we wouldn't be as good as the other communities. We wouldn't be as talented, our presentation wouldn't be

Big Creek High School homecoming parade float prepared and manned by Big Creek People in Action youth and adult fellows. Photo courtesy of Big Creek People in Action

as fun, and we just wouldn't be able to pull anything off.

I must tell you that the first meetings that were held to discuss what we could do for gifts for the other sites, and what we wanted to do for our presentation were truly tortuous!!! We tried everything to extricate ideas from the fellowship. We had circles, we wrote suggestions on paper and put them in a box, we tried to steal ideas from the Internet, we did everything we could think of, and we were getting nowhere fast. We had had several meetings and, so far, the only thing we could agree on was the fact that it was very important that whatever we did, we wanted it to be a representation of who we were and about our home. Finally, one of our adult fellows, Janis Hagy, came up with the idea of using the song "Country Roads." When she brought the suggestion up, the adults got very excited. We were just bouncing ideas around about it and felt so relieved that we finally had somewhere to start. *Then* we noticed the young'uns weren't saying much at all. When asked what they thought of the idea, they threw us for a loop! They asked what were we talking about—they had no idea what we were talking about and had never even heard the song. They were definitely NOT excited about doing "an old country" song, and one they knew nothing about.

Well, we left that meeting that night on that sour note. I discussed the issue with our youth co-coach, Alison Inman, the next day at work and as we talked we came to the realization that the two of us were a representation of the group of fellows—me (being an older fellow) being excited about the proposed presentation, and her (being a younger fellow) not being excited at all and not understanding why in the world we would even want to do such a presentation. Alison and I sat down and had a great discussion about why I liked the proposal and why she didn't. We decided neither one of us was right or wrong, but we were definitely on opposite sides of the fence. What we did decide, however, was that the discussion was great and that we should have all the fellows join in that discussion at our next meeting.

We started that next meeting with a circle, the subject being the pros and cons of the proposed presentation. Once this was finished, we realized it wasn't so much that the youth were dead set on NOT doing that particular song—it was just that they couldn't understand for the life of them **why** the song was important to the adult fellows and how it would represent our home, or how they could "identify" with the song. Of course, our next step was for the adult fellows to talk about what the song meant to them and why. There were some wonderful stories shared that night.

I told the story of being away from West Virginia for four years without coming home even once. When I did come home at the end of that four years' time frame, I remembered coming across Stony Ridge and having my stomach tied up in knots, because I could see home from the top of Stony Ridge. I had never, never realized what that would mean to me and how I would feel. *Then* to really stick it to me, the song "Country Roads" began to play on the radio. I literally had to pull over on the Horsepen turn and cry my eyes out. Pride, longing, joy, and regret—all of these emotions engulfed me. Home! Lord, I never knew it could mean SO much. I never knew I needed it SO bad. As I pulled back on the road and continued down the mountain, the song's words played in my head and I thought, "Yes, these country roads are taking me *home—to a place where I belong.*"

Next, Janis told the story of when she was a nurse in Vietnam and how much the song came to mean to her. She also told that it meant the same to every person in her unit, whether they were from the mountains of West Virginia or the flatlands of Indiana or the coast of South Carolina. It meant *home!* She told of when you are in a foreign country, witnessing the atrocities of war every hour of the day, never knowing from minute to minute if you would ever see your loved ones again—how then, can you even begin to imagine what the word home can come to mean to you?

Each adult had a story, a story of their own, as to why that song meant so much to them. Each story was as important and moving as the last.

This meeting turned into the longest meeting we had ever had, but no one seemed to be in a hurry to leave. No one was asking if the meeting was almost over. With each story shared, it seemed the room grew quieter. The young people were enthralled with the stories being told. They not only understood—they identified with the stories and the song.

Well, we had our song, but we also knew the young'uns were still feeling as though they didn't have as much input in the presentation. We tried to rearrange the song to make it "hipper." Rapping "Country Roads" just didn't come off very well! Finally, we decided to keep it the way it was with both adults and young'uns singing, but have the young'uns end the presentation with something that represented *them* and how they thought of home. We ended the presentation with the young'uns singing "We're From the Country, and We Like It That Way."

When we did our presentation at the gathering, we were nervous wrecks! All the other sites were so fantastic. Everyone from the other sites was SO talented—and then there was us. Absolutely no performing talent—one good singer (Bonnie Muncy) in the bunch—and, of course, she is also very timid and quiet—but we did have a true love for our home. We got up there in front of everyone and gave it our best shot and everything went great. Everyone from the other sites seemed to really enjoy it and everyone kept coming up to us the next day and singing lines from the song with us. Our own young'uns were so proud and they were singing the song on the airplane on the way home. The young'uns had taken ownership of that song and had so much pride about performing it. When we were back home the young'uns talked about the experience at school and we were asked to repeat the performance for the Board of Education's LSI meeting for the three high schools.

That is when we became partners. That is when we knew we could accomplish things *together.* That is when we learned to trust one another. Maybe a few years down the road, in another time and place, there will be a group of adults sitting around—and maybe one or two of those adults will have once been our youth fellows—and maybe they will be talking about the song "Country Roads." Perhaps they will share the stories that Janis, Rosetta, Rita, Darrell and I told about what the song meant to us. Maybe, just maybe, they will add another "Country Roads" story to the saga— maybe they will tell about the time in Olive Branch, Mississippi, when a group of young people and adults came together to sing a song about their work for community change and their youth/adult partnership, about how they felt about their place on earth, and what they learned about their heritage. I am sure—positively sure—they will tell the story with pride.

LIVING IN GRACIOUS SPACE

Earlier we talked about how nurturing relationships of trust makes it possible for those who have argued or been adversaries in the past to come together in common cause. We are very inspired by the story of the KLCC fellowship formed by the Salish Kootenai College in Ronan, Montana. They spent six months in the trust-building phase, using Gracious Space to develop a team. Their group included individuals recruited with the intention of reaching out to people who would not normally come together in that community. They united around a cause that they cared about more than past differences—education of their children.

Initially, the group's goal was to lower the 53 percent high school dropout rate of Native American youth in the Ronan School District. After six months of relationship building, the group changed their goal in response to what they had learned together. Their new goal was to improve the climate of the schools so all students would have a better opportunity to succeed.

This group of 28 fellows represented all parts of the community—teachers, college and high school students, school administrators, parents, local businessmen, and tribal leaders. Their coach, Harry Goldman, recalls, "At our first meeting we were all amazed at who was sitting in the room together engaged in civil dialogue .... Members of our fellowship come from both the Indian and the non-Indian groups, and under normal circumstances some of them would not choose to work together."

The group worked with the school district to create a welcoming school climate for families and students. Ideas that the group acted on included opening a family room so that Native American parents and students felt more at ease, starting a mentoring program for middle school students, finding ways to honor students, providing cross-cultural opportunities for students and parents, and performing myriad smaller activities. It was not easy and not done all at once. That, too, is a lesson of collective leadership.

When the KLCC program started, Julie was the only Native American employed in a professional position in the local school system. Even though the schools in Ronan were located in the heart of the Reservation, the principals, administration, teachers, and most of the school board came from the white part of the community.

At a meeting towards the end of the second year, Julie described her experience of working in Gracious Space. She shared how she initially found it difficult to be Gracious Space when she observed so many injustices around her; how hard it was to stay in Gracious Space when others did not offer it in return. Nevertheless, she committed to staying in Gracious Space, no matter how others might act. This eventually led to different relationships and different types of conversations, far more positive ones. She said that her experience became a journey from anger to hope.

We share this story about Julie because we vividly remember the meeting in which she told it. The meeting was in a room that represented the heritage of this particular Native American community. Over time, the room had been transformed into a community room for all, filled with so much love that we could feel it walking into the room. This story reflects the embodiment of relationship in action.

Earlier we also talked about how collective leadership can help individuals develop gifts and talents within the support of the group. All groups doing this work, including the Montana fellowship, have watched their members grow stronger as part of this process. In the following story, Mariah Friedlander describes what it was like to be part of such a group. She was fourteen years old when she joined the KLCC group. By age sixteen, Mariah was the first youth to be appointed to the Montana Indian Advisory Council on Education.

....

COMING TOGETHER
by Mariah Friedlander

A lot is going on in my life right now. I am getting used to being fully on my own—getting my own place, having a job. And I am proud to say that I am enrolled in the Airline Academy! I started being part of KLCC at age fourteen and I am twenty now.

You ask me what has stayed with me? Everything I did. I think my collective leadership experience influenced me to travel. It has influenced me to be aware of others' cultures and other people. Most of all, it has made me open-minded and open-hearted.

My Mom got me involved with this group. She would say, "You're coming with me. This is important." At the time, I didn't even realize how many opportunities I was being given, so many new experiences—meeting new people, traveling all over the country, flying by myself.

Interestingly, in some ways my involvement with KLCC made high school tougher for me because it gave me a mindset that was beyond high school.

Doing the collective leadership work, I was introduced to Gracious Space and leaders from around the country—each one respecting me, listening to me and valuing my opinions. My high school was like most other high schools—I did not feel my opinions were valued. With my KLCC family, everyone was so open-hearted and open-minded. It was a safe place for everyone to talk. A place I learned to be different. Some people were my age, but many were adults and we would sit around and talk about big issues—not just what was going on in my community, but all over the country. KLCC put me in a higher place—I felt like an adult. Being part of this group of people empowered me and also made me very humble.

When I was appointed to be on as state board for Indian education, I got a chance to see a very different kind of leadership. At the Indian Board meetings the feeling was, "We need to get this done." There was an intensity around having to make decisions and getting them pushed through. This was quite different from the Gracious Space of collective leadership where we would take the time to listen to each other—what each of us had to say was important—and as we sat and talked we would all be given leadership about what to do.

I remember the first KLCC meetings we had. Harry Goldman was our community coach and was leading those meetings. It was so intense because the room was filled with both Native Americans and non-Native Americans. There were so many strong feelings. Harry would let us get things off our

Mariah Friedlander (left) and her mother Anita Big Spring. Photo by Tony Lowe

chests and the tension would be so high—then Harry would make some remark that would make everyone laugh. And we could keep going.

How did that group turn into the KLCC family that I have been talking about? For me, the turning point when I felt we came together, when I remember being so happy and comfortable with each other, came at the first national gathering of communities in Chicago, toward the end of our first year of working together.

I remember we had to present our story to the whole group—people from all over the country. And before we went on, we had to figure out who was going to do what. Everyone was running around and not sure what was going to happen. Harry said, "All right, everyone, come together." He gathered us in a circle. He looked at us and said, "We will!" All of us then put our arms out into the middle of that circle, hands touching, and shouted, "We will!"

And that was the moment. That moment we all came together.

....

LONELY EYES
by Harry Goldman

I see the world through lonely eyes and feel the chill of winds
on time wrinkled cheeks

I take the steps that stomp and sometimes stagger but never lead to a
place of peace where contentment finds a quiet and gentle home

I struggle on
Driven by a ritual and rhythm that finds its beat in a hollow drum that
flies from harmony and distorts the sweet melodies that
warm the heart

I fall with desperation and despair landing on knees set for prayer
I throw a voice that cracks and quivers and hear an echo of hope
coming from souls united in spirit and purpose

I rise with the arch of the sun and no longer see my shadow
My reflection is found in the beings of fellows who spark the
inspiration and kindle the hope of life

Collective leadership fellows from Flathead Reservation in Montana. Photo by Jim Blow

Staying With It

As the stories in this chapter show, Gracious Space can become a powerful method for practicing the pattern of developing deep, trusting relationships that foster loving and supportive environments. Gracious Space is a very simple concept, but not one that is always easy to practice. Often, when conversations get hard, we step back into old patterns and habits of withdrawing or pretending that something will just go away. Gracious Space invites us to stay present when it most matters and offers us ways to work or even play through conflicts and disagreements.

This next story by Gayle de'Sousa Warner, a former vice-president at Mi Casa Resource Center for Women—now Mi Casa Resource Center— shares a difficult moment, the kind that occurs in every group that brings together people with very different life experiences. As this story reveals it is not always about what happens, it is about what happens next.

MOVING FROM JUDGMENT TO COMMITMENT
by Gayle de'Sousa Warner

I believed that after twenty-four years of working in the non-profit field I had become a great manager, rather good relationship builder, focused strategic planner, creative grant writer, and a supportive and caring colleague. I had also become someone who was more into outcomes and had little patience or appreciation for the process of reaching any outcome. I was most happy with results. I lived by these rules. Not to say that results don't have a place in our work lives, but to be completely obsessed, shall we say, by outcomes, is certainly a way to miss the general idea and mission of building stronger communities!

So, here I was when Mi Casa Resource Center for Women was awarded a grant to be one of the agencies in the Kellogg Leadership for Collective Change work. I was excited and open to the idea of working nationally with other very diverse communities. My job was to make sure we hit all the required outcomes so that we could be successful and look successful. I had no idea that this project would change my life.

We were all introduced to "Gracious Space" (I initially felt it was a throwback to the 1960s and a bit too funky) at the start of the project. I, like all good managers, read the book and was open to the idea of "inviting the stranger" and "learning in public." It took me a year or two into the process to realize that these are the key strategies to building deep relationships. I thought at first that these concepts were important, but did not realize how they would end up playing out in real life.

When we first met as a collective group of community members to work on community change, we wanted to make sure our group was diverse in every aspect and we did rise to this challenge. To give you an idea of the diversity, our group consisted of a school teacher, several college graduates, several inner-city youth, a couple of adults who were living below the poverty level, and several bi-cultural and bi-racial adults and youth. Our ages ranged from twelve years old to fifty-five or so! At first, we were eager to get to know one another, and were challenged to build a strong relationship as a group and as individuals to create change in our community.

I believed that we had successfully constructed deep relationships within the group. Then one day the agenda at our meeting was to look deeper at who we were by sharing some of our personal stories and beliefs. As we went around the circle (we were using circles as a way to communicate with one another for this exercise), a couple of individuals talked about their stories and these stories did not "land" well. The topic was around race and privilege, which can be an intense topic regardless of who is in the group, because we each come to the table with our own sets of values and beliefs.

It became apparent that this sharing offended several others in the group. I realized then that all of us had not done our inner-reflective work to challenge ourselves and our biases. I suppose at this moment I noticed the pain, which soon became anger projected out to the group. This of course changed the dynamics of the group for the worse. We had sidestepped what we had learned about being gracious and holding that as a way to behave with each other. I knew at this point that we needed to debrief and regain our trust in each other and then ask ourselves: "What happened?" "How could we move through this episode?" "What would it take?"

At this point, I also clearly understood that the concept of Gracious Space and the readings were important tools to hold onto, but that the hard work was for this to become a practice. If we wanted to move

A few of the collective leadership fellows from Denver, Colorado. Photo courtesy of Mi Casa

forward as a group, we would have to ask ourselves—over and over—if we would be able to learn in public and invite in the stranger once again. We took a break of sorts from one another to heal (some individuals missed a couple of meetings; others talked individually with some others about their feelings; one individual left the group while most everyone else came back to subsequent meetings).

I worked one-on-one with a couple of individuals trying to understand and listen to each story and each reality in each story. We debriefed and tried to identify why the message landed the way it did, and what would it take for each one of us to come back to the group to help move towards the group's healing. We did lose a few participants, but the majority were willing to continue the hard work and were committed to not only the change work, but the willingness to be open to others' ideas and to be respectful of different opinions.

As a year passed, I came to realize that we had built a strong group of people who wanted to do change work together. I, for one, realized that personal growth is ongoing and if we can have conversations to resolve any conflicts, then we can build a stronger dynamic within the established relationships. In my one-on-one conversations after the incident, I learned a bit more about each person, and some of the issues were worked out quickly while others needed more time. We were willing to do both.

For me this experience meant that I had become less judgmental, more compassionate and committed to relationship building as the foundation to community building.

....

CLOSING THOUGHTS

Developing relationships is the core work of collective leadership—relationships that allow us to be our best as individuals and as members of the group, relationships that allow us to engage the partners that will advance our change work. Many change processes focus on how others need to change in order for the community to be better served. One great benefit of collective leadership is that it invites us to look at ourselves, others, and the collective in dynamic new ways. Using Gracious Space encourages us to shift relationships with others by first living into how we want the community to be together. In this effort, we become more alive, present, and joyful with each other. From these types of connections and relationships, transformative change can and does emerge.

GOING HOME

by Shasta Cano
(performed by Shasta during a national gathering)

Going home, home, home
Almost home, home, home
Wanna go home, home, home
Almost home, home, home
Wanna go home

Driving onto the reservation
I just want to go home
Where it's safe and happy and I won't feel alone
Is it real? It's my ideal
'Cuz I know I can never go, never go back
As a child I would run and play
Safe guarded from day to day
And in my heart I knew
I could be a doctor, a lawyer, an artist & singer, too
I could fly high in the sky like superman and do what I want to do
I could be earth, wind or fire—All my heart's desires, I was free

Wanna go home, wanna go home,
Almost home, almost home
Feels like home, feels like home, wanna go home

You can go home if you choose
Home is now, home is you
Turn it around, that's all you gotta do
Going home, it's all about you

Wanna go home, wanna go home,
Almost home, almost home,
Feels like home, feels like home, wanna go home

CHAPTER TWO

CROSSING BOUNDARIES: WHAT CAN WE DO TOGETHER THAT WE CAN'T DO ALONE?

by Karma Ruder
with Saroeum Phoung, Misty Oldham, Cheryl D. Fields,
Sherry Timmermann Goodpaster, Liji Hanny, and
Victor Jose Santana

How does collective leadership support change that is beyond the reach of any one group?

In this chapter, we explore the second pattern of working together that collective leaders cultivate: **We cross boundaries that keep us from working with others who share our purpose,** *taking time to heal the hurts that remain from past differences. This enables us to join with those needed to take our work to its next level.*

As we let go of the limiting beliefs about ourselves and others that keep us from working together, our sense of inclusion increases and the social fabric becomes more closely woven, better able to keep us safe and warm.

This chapter, like the first, shares the stories of a diverse group of collective leadership practitioners, each in his/her own voice. It seems a fitting way to discuss the diverse boundaries we all face in this work. This chapter focuses on the challenges of moving across internal and external barriers that prevent us from doing the work we want to do, and reflects on how a boundary, re-imagined, can increase our capacity to serve our communities.

The Editors

Saroeum Phoung (holding feather) teaches peacemaking circles as a method to help people work through difficult conversations. Photo by Tony Lowe

As part of the national team, when we first visited a group ready to develop collective leadership, we began by cultivating relationship, listening to their stories, understanding their history and learning about their dreams. Then we would ask, "What is the boundary that you must cross in order for these dreams to become real? What limit have you accepted up to now that is getting in your way?"

We heard many thoughtful answers that included crossing racial barriers, reaching people in new geographic areas and thinking differently about who needed to be allies to advance the work.

One group in New Mexico included representatives from four different communities. Two of the communities were Native Americans who had been in their pueblos for a thousand years, and two were communities of the descendants of the conquistadors. This group was working to make the local high school a place that physically represented the cultures of all four communities because they were all sending their children to this school. This group also worked to make elementary and middle school better for students in the area by seeking ways for those schools to connect better with each other.

During an early retreat, people were exploring the question of boundaries. One Native American elder stood up and said, "We have been living side by side for centuries. Now it is time to realize that we need each other." This statement holds the essence of crossing boundaries.

To address the challenging issues facing our communities we must let go of old stories and limitations that keep us from collectively using all the talents and gifts available to us. Housing, education, healthy food, health care, and economic vibrancy, or its lack, are interconnected and require us to see the whole system. That is only possible when everyone contributes their vision, and that means we must work with those who are different from us, including those with whom we disagree. Though that is never easy, it is rewarding. It takes much energy to maintain a boundary. As we let go of a boundary, that energy is released and can be directed to finding creative answers.

In this chapter, we are going to explore many different kinds of boundaries. Any characteristic we embrace as making us unique and special (e.g., a particular heritage or experience) can also create a barrier that separates us from others who do not share that characteristic. Crossing boundaries requires that we first uncover assumptions we hold about others and ourselves, and then look to see if those assumptions are getting in the way of us effectively working together.

Before we can move to cross a boundary, we need to know our own boundaries, to have a clear sense of who we are and what we are bringing to an exchange. Having a clear identity creates deep supports that allow us to reach out, experiment with new relationships and take risks. Without those supports to hold us, a person or group can get lost when invited to cross boundaries. Knowing our heritage and having ties to a place provides stability and support when faced with challenges. Chapter 4 shares a profound story about how developing identity supports boundary crossing.

As human beings, we share the same fundamental needs and feelings. Sometimes what we have done to get our needs met has cost others in the community. When that has happened, people who have been hurt need time and space to heal. Otherwise, the depth of trust needed for working together towards common goals is not likely to be present. This healing process is an essential part of crossing some boundaries. Not addressing a need for healing can jeopardize our ability to move forward together. The story from the Lummi Nation makes this clear.

Even when we are committed to crossing boundaries, there are times it can feel like the process is asking too much of us. We have found that by identifying what we care about more than ourselves, we can stay engaged long enough to move across even difficult boundaries. The story from Buffalo is about this. There, a diverse group was willing to do the hard work of crossing racial boundaries because the participants kept focused on what they wanted to accomplish together. Their efforts produced great results for their community.

One of the rewards of crossing boundaries is what we learn about ourselves, others and our shared community. When we cross boundaries, we see that what is possible may be quite different from what we expected. As we begin to understand what life is like for others, we open up to the possibilities of what needs to be different, including adapting our own perceptions. The stories from Benton Harbor, Michigan, and Chelsea, Massachusetts, share some of the insights and some of the outcomes that can accompany this type of learning.

Collective leadership invites us to seek out those who share common purpose, to cross the boundaries that separate us—working through past hurts and forgiving each other—and then to work together in ways that fully respect all of those in the community. This can only happen when we are open to sometimes changing the ways we work with one another.

In Chapter 1, we offered Gracious Space as a methodology that helps a group develop deep relationships, which at times means moving across barriers that are excluding people from the group. Circle is another powerful approach that helps us work together in profound new ways and extends our notion of who we can work with successfully.

Roca Inc. has a longstanding and deep practice of using circle process in all their work. The circle process starts with knowing that while we all are part of a greater wholeness, our experiences sometimes cause us to forget that and feel broken. In circle, we restore each other and ourselves to our natural wholeness. In circle, we look at each other without the protection of desks or physical barriers, learn to make ourselves vulnerable, and see our wholeness. This is how boundaries can dissolve.

Roca has trained many other groups and communities in a circle process that dives deeply into the sacredness of relationship and community. They have generously provided a brief guide for working with circles that you will find in the Resources section. We have found we cannot do the hard work of crossing boundaries without the help of processes like Gracious Space and circle.

THE BOUNDARY WITHIN

When we have been hurt by how others have treated us, we may try to close off the wound by not looking at it. When we are in community, particularly when that community has a long history of oppression and discrimination, we can actually feel (even if we don't understand) the pain that has been experienced individually and collectively. Often, our first reaction to this pain is to back away because to look at it is so hard. Sometimes we are afraid that if we open up those past wounds, we will stay stuck in the pain and anger rather than moving through them to a stronger place. Buried pain sets up a boundary that exists within us.

As Saroeum Phoung, who leads and teaches peacemaking circles through his Point One North consulting firm, notes, we must stay present with our pain in order to move through the inner boundary that is keeping it contained. While working at Roca Saroeum learned from a Tagish Tlingit Chief how to practice circles as a sacred space. Saroeum names and honors this tradition whenever he leads a circle.

A few years ago the Lummi CEDAR project invited Saroeum to come to Washington and bring circle process to their community. The CEDAR Project staff knew that their community, as is true for communities of all cultures and heritages, had stories of pain and loss that would be hard to share. They knew that someone who did not know these stories first hand could ask questions and be witness in a way that could invite a new level of healing for the Lummi, a level that would enable them to advance their work. When CEDAR Project invited Saroeum, they took the risk that others in their community might question why someone from the outside should bring back to them a tradition of their own heritage. Crossing the cultural boundary that said outsiders should not hear their stories took great courage. In the end, everyone was honored and humbled by the depth of pain and by the depth of love and resilience that was shared.

YOU CAN'T GET TO A GOOD PLACE IN A BAD WAY
by Saroeum Phoung

When I was asked to introduce Peacemaking Circles to the Lummi living on the Lummi Reservation in Washington, I asked myself, "Who am I to share this process with them?" After all, circle is a part of Native American tradition and I am an outsider. And I answered, "Here I am."

People came because Tami and Shasta, both involved in CEDAR Project, invited them and the people trusted Tami and Shasta. Our aim was to have a group conversation—a dialogue with everyone—to start a healing process. For two years, I went back and forth, meeting with different groups of Lummi. Each of the four times I visited them, I conducted four-day circles.

What follows are my notes on my time with the Lummi. What the Lummi have achieved is such a positive example of something I always say: "You can't get to a good place in a bad way."

FIRST CIRCLE: Circle training in July of the first year for twelve to fifteen people.

In the room are a mixture of people, some who are Lummi and some who are not. They all sit in the same room and in circle. This is the first time for them to speak their minds and to listen to each other voice their concerns and express their views and perspectives. People are sharing their stories, history, frustrations, and the harm that has been done to them—all that is part of the Lummi environment today.

The circle is focused on healthy communication and creating space for everyone to be who they are and accept their own truths. This opens everyone to understanding and acknowledging the feelings that reflect the entire community's current reality. At this meeting, we address the tension in the room and take the first step toward healing and understanding. We talk about what individuals need to do—including taking ownership of what they need to do—to make things better and to focus on now, not on what happened in the past. Focusing on now is the beginning step to make things better for individuals and for the community. This is the first time that this group of Lummi has engaged in these types of dialogue.

My personal lesson: So much has been done to and taken from the Lummi Nation.

Lessons learned by the group: In the beginning, there was an uneasy feeling. The Lummi have so many underlying issues as well as symptomatic issues to deal with. Their story is a cycle of oppressions with resulting deep-rooted conflicts and trauma. The Lummi are struggling with wanting to live the Lummi way, but what that means and how they can do it are huge challenges—it is not so easy to keep in sight who they are and where they came from.

I shared a story of young men I used to work with and a story from my own past—young Cambodian men who had to deal with racial violence on a regular basis. Our lack of understanding of racial profiling and the ongoing language barrier left us confused and angry. As parents, too, we were lost and didn't know how to support our own children.

For those of us who are children of war and who have had to face violence on a daily basis and witness first hand that violence, the racial violence reminded us of the feelings and actions of those wartimes. We began to organize, figuring out ways to protect ourselves and our families from the racial violence that impacted our daily lives. We fought back, using violence against violence. We began to reenact the violence taught to us and to relive the drama and rage.

For a few years, this went on. Eventually, most of our enemies were sick of us and the violence, and they began to move out and to disappear. But by now the group had expanded and the anger was at its peak among young Cambodian men and women alike. With no enemy in sight, soon we began to clash with each other, fighting with each other. There were more and more gangs, creating intense rivalry. We had completed one cycle of oppression, only to have a new cycle of self-destruction begin yet again.

Trusting each other and relationships with each other were essential because all outsiders are seen as the enemy. This is also the case of the Lummi, rightfully so—so many outsiders have done and taken so much from them. In the Lummi history, there are clear scars that have deeply affected them and have become part of the Lummi way—what is important now is to be open to things just as they are.

SECOND CIRCLE: Circle training in April of the second year for forty to sixty people.

This circle has the biggest group of people participating in the circle process ever. This has a lot to do with how Misty and Shasta have encouraged the elders, adults, and young people, all who are very connected to CEDAR Project, to come to this circle. Elders were invited to help lead in the opening ceremony and many elders shared traditional stories with the group. Many people expressed that they had never heard some of these stories before. They shared their concerns about these stories being lost and the importance of sharing these stories with everyone, especially the young people who are the future leaders of the Lummi Nation.

Throughout the first and second days of this second circle process, many adults and elders shared and expressed their views and perspectives. Elders shared their deepest concern about being alone and their feeling that no one really cares about them, and that this was never the Lummi way. They said that the wisdom of oral storytelling holds within it the wisdom of the Lummi elders. Most of the elders were also expressing their concern that the young people were not talking—most just saying one or two words and passing the talking piece.

Then, at the end of the second day, the young people spoke just a little bit more. A few said that many elders never allow their young ones to speak freely. Oftentimes, the young ones have to ask to speak and most of the time they never have the chance to really communicate their views and get their perspectives across. On the third day of the circle training, many young people began to speak from their hearts and express very similar feelings to the ones the elders expressed—feelings that no one really cares about them, that they feel alone and isolated in their own environment.

Others who were in the circle but not Lummi then shared their feeling of not being a Lummi but just an outsider. They talked about how they were treated and the uncomfortable feeling of wanting to help and yet not feeling sure if they were accepted in the Lummi community, or if they were respected for who they are.

Lots of issues were out in the open and everyone seemed to be okay, and to acknowledge that these ways are not good for them and for the Lummi as a Nation. They expressed their individual willingness to help resolve these issues and to make the Lummi a better striving community. Some offered to help host circles with young people at the CEDAR Project, to help host circles with elders at the CEDAR Project and, most importantly, to host a monthly circle gathering to keep the fire going and to continue the dialogues.

THIRD CIRCLE: A keepers' circle training in June of the second year for ten to fifteen people.

A circle training of keepers ends as a deep healing circle, as we go through many layers of feelings, as in peeling an onion. A keepers' circle is always a small group focusing on deepening relationships and the healing process. It requires pushing everyone to deal with and confront their own personal difficult issues and their own personal development. The intensity of personal sharing among our small group, the risks taken, and the courage of individuals telling for the first time their own stories that have not been shared before is remarkable. Some of the stories have been hidden for twenty years, some more than sixty years. For so long, people have carried the secrecy of personal victimization (the trauma of hiding ourselves from everyone and yet always expecting to be found out).

The keepers' training is focused on personal healing and development. This is a continuous process so that the keepers of the circle process don't get in the way of others or themselves. The keepers are ideally serving and honoring the circle process. We share our own stories as a way to encourage others to speak, so that others feel invited to speak, not controlled or forced. The notion is that we cannot lead where we do not dare to go ourselves—being a keeper of the circle requires that you share only yourself and your personal story.

As keepers we invite others to share the stories that they feel comfortable with sharing. This happens through relationship building and trust building, and care is taken that only when the time is right will a story be shared. These stories should be shared without rushing or pressing an individual to share anything that that person is not ready to share. It is not about the keeper's individual gain, and keepers must always be careful not to impose their own agenda or get in the way of the other participants in that circle. This keepers' circle training was one of the deepest circles that I have been to, and I have been to or hosted a few thousand circles.

FOURTH CIRCLE: In September of the second year, eighteen to twenty-five people came to a circle for the purpose of designing a custom program, building a working committee, and planning work.

This circle with the Lummi Nation tribal court included more than twenty professional organizations. Its purpose was to figure out the needs and core values of each organization, and then come up with ways in which they could help each other achieve shared objectives by performing their own individual duties. They wanted to use circle to find alternative ways to work with youth who have gotten into trouble.

So far, they have worked on a channeling process and procedure to

Lummi CEDAR Project collective leadership fellows. Photo courtesy of Lummi CEDAR Project

address what will happen to these youth. The system they have come up with is legally compliant yet flexible enough to allow the community and involved organizations to provide input to the decision-making process by expressing their views and perspectives.

They also have been setting up a committee that will act as a leadership team and take on the daily responsibility and workload of educating the community about the circle process and its benefits. One benefit is capacity building—more people are willing and better able to help with the work. The committee will perform circle training, including Keepers' Training, and make sure that everyone who is interested in the circle process has access to it. This includes making people familiar with circle terminology and principles. The next circle at Lummi will focus on reflection: What has been learned in this journey of bringing circle back into the Lummi Nation? Stories about this will be gathered to use as part of the evaluation process, and also to provide documentation that can be shared with others.

I want to thank everyone who has made this happen. A few people are Shasta, Misty, Ron, Juanita, and Jason. I want to acknowledge the willingness to trust the circle process and to trust each other. Together we have put a dream into practice. I want to thank the Tagish Tlingit for sharing their knowledge and wisdom with me so I could bring it here. It is important to honor both the Tagish Tlingit and the Lummi for sharing their stories.

....

What the Lummi and those of us who have worked with Saroeum have learned is that the work of crossing boundaries requires returning again and again to the issues that challenge us. Even though we all instinctively look for a quick fix to our problems, we cannot rely on one interaction or one moment of clarity to resolve feelings and experiences that have been created over a long time. Instead, we need to change our habits to shift the dynamics of how we get together.

As Saroeum tells us, "The process of being in circle creates a realistic way to not rush to the issues so we can hear and understand each other. Only then can we begin to understand our relationship to the issue that brought us together and to other issues. With circle, we *arrive* at the issues we need to address. We have talked and listened to each other and then know the issues—they emerge from the conversation.

"If we don't create a place for healing then we aren't nurturing the relationship. Healing is never just one time. We are energies coming together. We are imperfect human beings. To be holistic, we have to embrace all of us—spiritually, mentally, physically—even the hurtful broken things about us. If we don't transform the anger and the pain, we transfer them."

Saroeum's support of the Lummi Nation's work to transform their historic pain has had a continuing impact on that community. Here, Misty Oldham shares what that means from the perspective of someone from within the Lummi community. Misty Oldham first connected to CEDAR Project as a youth in the Summer Leadership Institute, and then as a youth evaluator for KLCC. She is now the staff person leading the organization's Youth Leadership Institute.

....

CREATING A SAFE SPACE
by Misty Oldham

I have been working at the Lummi CEDAR Project (LCP) for the past eight years. I have witnessed many changes within the organization, some good, and some not so good. One of the most beneficial tools that we adopted is the Peacemaking Circles (PMC) process. Through PMC, we found a healthier way to communicate with one another to build stronger relationships within the organization and community; most importantly, we found a way of creating Gracious Space for everyone to share their story in a safe environment.

The PMC is an ongoing process—it takes time to build trust with yourself and others. As people are sharing something openly and honestly within a group setting, it may feel like others have access to see one another's weaknesses and/or vulnerability. It is important to remember we are all in our own levels of personal growth and understanding, and resolving our own issues is not always easy. In some cases, PMC provides the chance for the storyteller to heal, to release feelings that may have been bottled up for a long time. Also, the sharing of stories gives everyone an opportunity to learn from one another.

PMC provides the time and space to sit down and give everyone a chance to ask ourselves questions, for example, "What is the real reason why I'm upset?" and "What are the next steps I can take to better the situation?" When we take the time to listen to ourselves, it helps us to identify our individual needs as well as to understand what others are going through.

Lummi CEDAR Project's Misty Oldham (right) and Carmen Bland. Photo courtesy of the Lummi CEDAR Project

In the past two years, I found it difficult when serious issues were brought up, yet I have learned a lot through the process of PMC; from these experiences I have gained some insight about how important it is to hear each other out in a healthy and safe manner, rather than ignore the issue.

I remember a situation where staff members were getting upset with one another, so we called an emergency PMC, sat down, talked about what it is we were frustrated with, and towards the end we all came to middle ground. There was one thing that worried us; our new staff member was quiet throughout the PMC. We were worried that we frightened her with our actions, so we asked her if there was something wrong. She said there was nothing wrong, and she was shocked to see how we came together as adults to talk out an issue in a healthy way. She mentioned that the only way her family dealt with conflict was by either ignoring the situation or being bad-mannered. She thanked us for showing her a healthier way of communicating.

Most times in the past, when there was a problem, the problem would not go away—the people would. Today, we practice PMC. It has given us a way to talk directly with each other, in a respectful manner, and it helps us work together in a good way.

Over time, we learned that being "in circle" isn't always done in an actual physical circle, but an invisible one, too. As Saroeum says, "Staying in circle, when not in circle." If there is a problem and someone tells you how they feel, say thank you for sharing your point of view, and share yours as well. It is important to not only talk but to listen as well, and vice versa.

There was another time when we were in a transitional process within the organization, and there were some growing pains that included a challenging lesson. We needed to unlearn unhealthy behaviors that were so entrenched within the organization. There was a time when a co-worker and I were pretty upset with each other, and were both afraid to say what was on our minds. Finally I said, "We know about peacemaking circles. Let's go through the process—even though it's not so much a circle." One question we kept in mind was, "Well what does staying in circle, when not in circle mean?" We decided that perhaps it means living by the principles of circular communication—having an open-mind, listening to each other's stories, and checking in with one another when we can, at home or work.

One of the key points that I've learned about circle so far is being the example, using the process in your own life at work or at home. To be able to talk about circle you have to be living it. And another point is that it is important to create Gracious Space from the beginning. If we wait until it's needed, then it's too late.

....

In the same way that both Saroeum and Misty make clear that the crossing of boundaries is never a one-time-and-it's-done effort, they also remind us that there is never just one boundary—one idea, experience, or point of view—that needs crossing in order to live our lives fully or to do our work.

THE BOUNDARY BETWEEN
The next story tells about the crossing of a boundary that perhaps every American has at sometime needed to cross—the boundary of racial differences. In many of our communities, this boundary is deep-seated and is particularly challenging.

ON THE ROAD TO A POST-RACIAL AMERICA
by Cheryl D. Fields

The week before Barack Obama was elected president of the United States, I attended a Democratic Party rally in northern Virginia. It would be Obama's last public appearance as a candidate and it was the eve of what a few naive observers dubbed the dawn of America's post-racial period.

The rally was held at a county fairground and was attended by one of the most culturally diverse crowds of which I have ever been part. There was an invigorating feeling of camaraderie on the lawn that evening as we sang, danced, chanted, and laughed together for hours while waiting for the candidate to appear. Twice, however, our festive fellowship was threatened by the racially insensitive actions of a few participants.

The first episode involved a young white woman who appeared to be in her twenties. She and a handful of white male friends were standing about twenty yards in front of me. From time to time, the tallest of the guys would hoist her onto his shoulders so that she could display a hand-made, pro Obama banner. Scrawled across the paper in brightly colored paint were the words "Obama, I Want to Have Your Baby." Many of the people around me remarked that the banner was in poor taste. Others complained that it was obscuring their view of the podium.

My first reaction to the poster was outrage. How dare she come into a public space and so directly disrespect this married black man and his family. To make it worse, she was cute, young and white, just the sort of woman many African American mothers caution their newlywed daughters to beware lest their husbands be lured astray. In retrospect, I realize that the woman probably never anticipated the impact her sign would have on someone like me. She thought she was paying Obama a compliment. The painful history of African American women being characterized as less desirable than their white peers, and of the countless African American men who were routinely lynched for daring to look at a white woman, as well as the ongoing struggle of African American couples to establish and maintain healthy marriages probably never entered her mind.

Still, as the hours wore on, I became aware that I was not the only one for whom the sign had struck a racial nerve. Several women of color in the audience began verbalizing their disapproval of the banner. One

Latina, who was accompanied by her pre-teen son, bent my ear for several minutes expressing her disapproval. "Obama is such a positive father figure for our young people," she said. "And here this chick comes with this sign to totally disrespect his children and his beautiful wife. I'm so sorry my son has to see this. It's embarrassing!"

Eventually, several of the women near me began shouting at the young woman to put the banner down. Fortunately, she and her buddies put away the sign before the harsh words escalated into violence.

Later in the evening, a separate trio of young white women got into a heated exchange with a young black woman who complained about their cigarette smoking. Even though race had little to do with the situation, racial insults were exchanged. Ultimately, a pair of older women in the crowd persuaded the squabbling youth to calm down and remember why they had come to the rally, which they did.

As I watched these events unfold, I thought about the hundreds of episodes I've experienced over the course of my life in which racial, cultural and other social tensions boiled just below the surface. Left to escalate, many have ended in violence. The difference between the Obama rally and these other episodes was the Obama crowd's shared allegiance to a common objective. I have seen it before—when culturally diverse groups join together to address a community issue, their shared interest in that issue can help people work through racial tension.

It is also beneficial to have a process for acknowledging racial/cultural differences as we move toward change. Too often, communities don't have such a framework at their disposal. A sequence of events occurring in Buffalo, New York, during the past decade, offers an explicit example of how the collective leadership process can provide such a framework.

The Boundaries We Carry With Us

In 2002, Buffalo was listed among the top ten most racially segregated cities for African Americans in a report released by the U.S. Census Bureau.[1] At the time, the city's school district ranked among the lowest in the nation, and it had a double digit rate of unemployment. That same year, the W.K. Kellogg Foundation selected Buffalo as one of six communities nationwide to participate in its new initiative, Leadership for Community Change (KLCC).

The first time I met the Buffalo KLCC fellows was at a national gathering in Itasca, Illinois. Their group, which was split more or less evenly

---

1 U.S. Census Bureau. (2002). "Racial and Ethnic Segregation in the United States, 1980-2000." U.S. Department of Commerce, Economics & Statistics Administration, pg. 28

between whites and people of color, the latter of whom were mostly African Americans, had already been working together for several months. I was part of the communications team hired by Kellogg to work on the KLCC project. As I sat at a table with this group on the first day, I could tell they enjoyed each others' company. By the end of the gathering, based on snippets of their conversation and certain body language, I could also see that issues around race and culture, if not thoroughly addressed, would limit what they would be able to accomplish together. I was not alone in this view.

Years later, Dr. Danis Gehl, the group's local site evaluator, told me that one of her initial observations of the Buffalo fellows was that they had conflicting expectations for the program, some of which were connected to racial and cultural differences. "Their ideas about leadership...—some of which had to do with the diversity of the group—struck me as very different," she said.

It was a collective leadership storytelling project that brought Buffalo's racial boundary out into the open. In preparation for that first national gathering, each of the KLCC sites was asked to prepare a presentation that would introduce their community to the other fellows. The Buffalo fellows and their host agency, the Public Policy and Education Fund's Citizen Action of New York (Citizen Action), opted to tell the story of their community in a photo and video presentation. When the video was shown to the Buffalo group, prior to the national gathering, there was strong disagreement about the way some ethnic and cultural communities were depicted. At that point, the fellowship used Gracious Space and other collective leadership tools to focus on their shared purpose and on how they could work together with a deeper appreciation of each other.

During the process of making the video presentation, the group learned a lot about each other, including just how much race, class, gender, and other social characteristics influenced each one's experience of Buffalo.

"I think that the decision to bring the video story to the national gathering, in spite of the really fresh wounds that the episode had caused within the fellowship, demonstrated the group's understanding that not only did they need to address issues brought to light by this situation, but that addressing the issue was a critical part of the collective leadership process," Danis said.

The Sweet Rewards Of Crossing Racial Boundaries

The fellows' awareness that they had to address their differences before they could accomplish their goals became an essential piece of their continuing effort to work together in new ways. As a result of this effort the Buffalo group began to effectively tackle the issue of racial equity in education. They were able to attract more than $1.5 million in after school funding for their community—a huge increase from the $150,000 of the year before. They mobilized local Latino residents to engage in the political process and, through a voter education campaign, persuaded disaffected residents that their votes could make a difference. The voters responded by electing an entire new slate of school board members.

As dramatic as these results were, what has proven most significant and enduring are the ways of working together that this group have introduced to their community. Members of the Buffalo fellowship say the collective leadership principles, introduced to the group early on, helped them to respectfully acknowledge the boundaries of race, culture, and class that separated them, while also helping them to identify their shared goals and values. The experience opened them up to learn from one another, and gave them a process for collectively pursuing their goals. As the Buffalo group crossed the boundary of their racial and ethnic differences, they used their newfound coalition to pursue racial justice.

Ceylane Meyers, then deputy director of the Buffalo chapter of Citizen Action, served as the group's community coach. Inspired by what she saw happening in Buffalo because of Citizen Action's boundary-crossing work, she went to the statewide organization and invited them to use Gracious Space as a way to examine how they were operating, specifically how they selected which actions to pursue across the state. She invited them to look at their own behavior in contrast with their stated goals. What the organization discovered was that its process for selecting which issues to address was unintentionally biased towards the white decision makers. Once they realized this, they shifted their decision-making process to reflect their belief in inclusiveness and service to those most vulnerable. They transformed the entire statewide agency to more intentionally acknowledge race as they pursued their civic justice work.

"We looked at our issue campaigns in a totally new way, reframing them from the perspective of racial equity. ... We [also] approached leadership development in a more explicit, more structured, and more practical way. These two organizational changes are very interconnected. The focus on structural and institutional racism, combined with intensive leadership development work through our issue campaigns, will enable us to build a multi-racial leadership group that goes beyond the 'crossing boundaries' of KLCC to a shared commitment to fight for racial justice and racial equity in all of our work." (Citizen Action report to W. K. Kellogg Foundation)

Citizen Action has since developed an interracial racial justice team within the organization to direct its commitment to fighting racism. The organization also hired two new senior staff members who have the skills to work on leadership development, staff development, and infusing racial justice goals into the work. This means they've been able to sustain and expand their racial justice work even though Ceylane left the organization a few years ago to pursue a new job in the state legislature.

For KLCC fellows John Calvin Davis, an African American attorney, and Fabiola Friot, a Colombian immigrant and local social worker, the collective leadership work across boundaries marked a new experience. Both had had prior experiences working in racially diverse groups, but the KLCC experience was unique because it openly acknowledged racial and cultural differences and provided a framework for people to identify and pursue shared goals despite their differences.

"The work that we've done has helped us to drop some of the barriers that existed between us when we initially gathered," John said during a video interview a few years ago. "Normally, people would expect a group of young black professionals, for example, to come together and do a presentation on racial disparities in education. Now, all of a sudden the fellows walk in and they are young, old, short, tall, black, and white. It has really opened up the city's eyes."

Fabiola took what she learned about crossing boundaries within the KLCC fellowship and applied it to the complex cultural landscape of Buffalo's Latino community, which includes Puerto Rican Americans and immigrants from Central America, Cuba, and Mexico.

"The Hispanic population in Buffalo [was] totally disenfranchised," she said during an interview videotaped several years ago. "The saying is that [in] the Hispanic community, the people don't get along, they end up fighting with each other and nothing gets accomplished. I was determined that I was going to bring Hispanic leaders together."

And, by bringing boundary-crossing work into her community, she did. The Latino coalition Fabiola spearheaded opened the door for Ralph Hernandez to become Buffalo's first Latino member of the school board. At the time of this book's printing, he was beginning his third term and was serving as the board's president.

The KLCC initiative in Buffalo came to an end a few years ago. Although the fellows have disbursed, most remain active in civic affairs and the cross-cultural relationships they formed continue to serve the community.

"For example," Danis says, "when the local commission on human rights was reorganized, John Calvin Davis was tapped to be its chair. He immediately looked out and said, "Who are some people that I know

Buffalo collective leadership fellows. Photo by Cheryl D. Fields

who will bring fresh perspective to this work?" And while it wasn't in the realm of education, he reached out to two of the former fellows to see if they would become part of the commission, which they did."

Like many Americans, I scoff at the notion that our nation has reached a post-racial period. Neither Buffalo, nor even the Buffalo fellowship, have arrived at that state. Still, as a result of the collective leadership experience, today Buffalo is a city where a committed band of collective leadership practitioners have the skills, experience, and relationships needed to cross racial boundaries in pursuit of a more equitable community.

I'm not sure what a post-racial America looks like. But I am convinced that collective leadership across racial boundaries is an essential lane on the road that will get us there.

....

Sherry Timmermann Goodpaster, executive director of New Paradigm Partners Inc., works with a boundary commonly separating rural communities—the boundary of geographic distance. It takes a great deal of patience to bring together communities that are geographically far apart, communities similar and yet each with its own unique perspective. Sherry's story illustrates what often happens when a boundary that separates two groups is viewed with a new outlook—it is transformed into an asset.

GOING THE DISTANCE
by Sherry Timmermann Goodpaster

New Paradigm Partners Inc., (NPP) is located in the north woods of Wisconsin. Our area is a beautiful, pristine part of Wisconsin. With a lake around every corner, a forest thick with pines and hardwoods, and rolling hills, it is known as the Blue Hills of Wisconsin. We are rural, very rural. With only two students per square mile, we have more deer per square mile than students. Unemployment is higher than the state average and household income lags behind the state average as well. The school district is one of the largest employers in our communities, and also provides many of the social opportunities in our communities. If you tell someone you've got tickets to the game, it means you are going to the high school football game; going to the theater is the school play, and going to a concert is the local school band concert.

NPP's vision is networking small communities through learning. When we say small, we mean an average population of around 500–1000. The eight school districts that have joined together to make up NPP are spread over an area of 2,000 square miles. That means sometimes people drive as much as two hours to get to a gathering.

The original intention of forming NPP was to find ways for all the schools to share resources and information, and to create strong bonds between schools and communities. The idea has always been for both the community and the schools to understand the role and impact of schools in the community, and to understand how to partner.

NPP received the Kellogg Foundation grant during a time of transition when a new executive director was coming in. All the people hired to work with KLCC were committed to improving the community and to advancing adult learning—and they were new to community work. Some of the early projects veered away from NPP's mission to strengthen the bond between schools and community. When I was hired as executive director in the second year of the program, it was in part because of my experience in community work and also because of NPP's desire to return to the original focus on community and school partnership.

Even as we were in the process of sorting through how to make sure that the collective leadership projects were in line with the original purpose of NPP, I was seeing benefit from the new way the communities were learning together. The collective leadership process invited us to take the time to do relationship building, and that meant that the communities began to know each other and trust each other. This was essential, particularly since the geographic distances we all have to deal with felt like such a challenge.

I first noticed at the national gatherings for KLCC how helpful it was for everyone from different communities to meet each other, how people returned home inspired with new ideas and new enthusiasm. Then I noticed that the same thing was happening in our communities. The geographical distances that are a part of our lives were no longer just a challenge. They had become an asset to our work. Being the only small community within thirty or forty miles can feel so isolating. When we got together to do our work, we were pulled out of our own way of looking at various problems. We would go home with new ideas and energy.

So, at NPP, we really focused on how viewing distance as an asset could make our programs stronger. One ongoing program we offer gives teachers a chance to meet with others who teach similar subjects; for example, science and math teachers might get together to exchange ideas about what they are doing in the classroom. We always do team-building at these meetings so that these gatherings go beyond just a superficial exchange of information. Our teachers are forming their own community as well as seeing themselves as part of the community at large. As a result, our members now look forward to these opportunities to get together with the shared purpose of making their individual schools stronger.

Another way we are extending what we have learned about sharing across distance is a program we recently started for middle-schoolers. The program responds to the age old complaint of youth in small towns, "There's nothing to do." We asked the question of the youth in each town, "Well, what is there to do? What is an asset in your community that you can invite others to come and see?"

Each group of youth came up with something fun and unique about their home town and then invited the youth from all the surrounding communities to come spend a day with them. Birchwood has a park and swimming beach and a great ice cream parlor that they showcased. The New Auburn youth planned their day around an interpretive center that has trails that follow the movement of ice during the ice age in Wisconsin. Shell Lake, the largest of our communities, has its own mini-airport and so the Shell Lake youth featured learning about aviation. Local pilots volunteered to take youth up for airplane rides. We loved the fact that pilots have to have a clean record to be able to get their

Wisconsin collective leadership fellows. Photo by Elizabeth Bettenhausen

pilot license, because that reinforced our ongoing effort to have youth stay away from drugs and alcohol. During each of these days, we had fun and we shared a circle so people could learn something new and often meet someone new.

Of course, getting to where we are now was not easy or quick. We had to learn the lesson that not everyone is ready for the hard work of relationship building and crossing boundaries. To do this work, you have to be open to working in a new way. I am always looking for new people to invite into our work. I look for people who are kind and able to trust. I look for people willing to focus on cross-community issues. Some individuals are so focused on themselves that having them at meetings is counterproductive. Once you make collective leadership the way your community works together, you are always inviting people to step up and grow. And you have to know that there are always some people who prefer to just step away; that is okay.

When I look back on my time with New Paradigm Partners Inc., I can see how far we have come. All our communities have come a long way with collective leadership. The youth participation, in particular, has been amazing to watch grow.

We have learned that it takes time to build trust and that trust comes at different times for different folks. This work requires patience! Even now, when we have become so comfortable with the principles of collective leadership, I can see that our relationships continue to deepen and that people come on board with an ever greater sense of partnership.

Many of our original fellows in this work have moved on, some to elected office and some to other work that can use these lessons. Yet even as people have come and gone, the work has been sustained—both in how we do our work in community and through continuing programs. The school store that was started as a practical learning experience is still operating, as are several of the programs that were started to better connect parents to the schools. And, for us in the beautiful Blue Hills of Wisconsin, this work has lessened the hardships and isolation of geographic distances, and strengthened the powerful energy of community.

....

A boundary that we all must cross is the one of age. As is clear from stories throughout this book, we believe that true collective leadership is cross-generational. During KLCC, we explored youth and adult partnerships as a powerful way to advance just communities.

What we have learned is that sometimes it is hardest to see the potential in, and to be open with, those who are closest to us! While youth also have to be willing to hear adults in different ways, it is often much harder for adults to unlearn behaviors that repeat how they were treated by adults when they were young, even if those behaviors weren't particularly helpful—then or now.

Liji Hanny from the Boys and Girls Club of Benton Harbor fully lives into unlearning his old behaviors and embracing youth and adult partnerships in a very profound way. While that quality was reflected in his story in Chapter 1 about deepening relationships, the following story focuses on one of the toughest parts of youth and adult partnership for many adults—truly sharing decision-making. One way to know whether or not you have genuinely crossed a boundary is to ask yourself—are you willing to share power?

THE POWER OF INTERGENERATIONAL PARTNERSHIPS
by Liji Hanny

It was really hard for me in the beginning to shift from our model of mentoring young people to being their partners. But once I did, everything changed. I had to learn that if I wanted the youth to embrace change and take risks, then I had to embrace change and take risks. If I wanted them to be good partners, then I had to be a good partner and let them make decisions—and then back them up.

Early up, I was very humbled by a conversation I had with one of our youth. She had been let down by a lot of adults and she really let me have it about what I was saying and whether I was going to be any different. I let myself get really hot in that conversation and then I was very humbled by what she said and by how I had not modeled what I had been telling her. When I went back to apologize, she told me it had been helpful to be challenged about her assumptions. What she taught me is that you have to lead, follow or get out of the way. For a lot of young people, adults just get in the way. They don't lead and they don't follow. They just want to question whatever it is that young person wants to do and to tell her that that isn't the way it's done. If a young person has an idea, you need to support it and get behind it or you need to get out of the way and let him try it.

A simple request for furniture became a watershed moment in coming to understand this.

We quite often get second-hand furniture donated to us. By the time it comes to us, it is usually already torn, or marked up, or even a little broken. With regular use, most of the furniture we get would have about six months' life in it. But, of course, the furniture at the Boys and Girls Club gets really heavy use, so the life of the furniture is even shorter.

One day, a piece of furniture broke and a teen said, "When are we going to get a piece of furniture that we get to mark on ourselves? When are we going to have something that we can say, 'Yes, I was here. I saw when that leg got scratched or broken'?"

This started a discussion. The young people said they wanted to buy new furniture because everything here was beat up and shabby and it didn't make them feel respected.

Then the group of teens turned to me and said, "Can't getting new furniture be part of our collective leadership project?"

I said I didn't know and I took that request to the rest of the staff. The staff said it was a bad use of money to buy new furniture because it wouldn't last and then the money would be gone. They said, "They're just going to tear it up." I replied, "If they tear it up, at least it's theirs to tear up. Why should they have to live with furniture that got torn up by others?"

I thought that would not be accepted but, in fact, it was the end of the discussion. The next question was, "Will the grant pay for it?" And it would. We did some focus groups to find out what the teens wanted. A store that had donated furniture in the past gave us information on choices and we created a diagram of the space and figured out what would fit in which rooms. The youth picked out the furniture and the colors. When it was time to buy, Erica, one of the youth fellows, went with me. Almost as soon as we arrived, I got called away. When I came back, Erica had made all the purchases and I just had to sign off.

That was a turning point for big decisions at the teen center—no more decisions without the youth being part of it.

When we bought that furniture, it made a huge difference. It was what the teens wanted and it made them feel good to be in a place that was comfortable and had good furniture. Other teens came in and saw nice stuff. And the cool part was their peers had picked it out.

At the teen center, our numbers just kept going up. We had a lot more young people coming to the teen center when they found out it was a place where they could be part of making decisions about what they would do and how it would be done.

When we got to the third year of doing our collective leadership work, we were on our fourth Executive Director. He came over to the Teen Center and he said he didn't understand what this whole collective leadership youth-and-adult-partnership approach was but he could feel and see the difference. He wanted that same feeling over in the main building with all of our programs.

So, I got promoted to Director of Operations to bring all that learning over to the main building. I brought some youth to take a lead at the main center to carry over the Teen Center approach. It's hard for some of the staff. I come in and want them to be different, even with the very young ones. Instead of programming everything for them, I tell them let's create some spaces where the youth can make some of their own decisions about what they are going to do. I hear a lot that this isn't the way we do it and I know that to get them to come on board I have to just keep modeling it and embracing change and taking risks.

As for me, I've known some of these youth since they were ten or eleven, and seeing them grab the reins is so cool. Youth and adult partnering is time-consuming, but the impact on all involved is so great. It's like being born again.

....

The boundary of age highlights a challenge to crossing boundaries that is often missed—first you have to recognize that there is a boundary that needs crossing!

In the case of working with youth, we often think of them as individuals who, one day, will be leaders but who, for now, need a lot of direction and a lot of rules. Once we cross the boundary of age—with all its assumptions about how adults are supposed to teach and youth are supposed to learn—we can begin to see youth as today's leaders, who, as they lead, are developing and refining their skills and capacities. It is important, and not always easy, to connect youth to change work in real ways that honor their gifts of insight and their natural ability to question the status quo.

THE BOUNDARY LEFT BEHIND

The final story in this chapter on crossing boundaries comes from Roca in Chelsea, Massachusetts. As you will see, Roca's youth and adult partnerships work for systemic change and are addressing questions of policy related to immigration. Though Roca is committed to crossing the boundary of age in their work, we offer the following story to make a different point. The story from Roca is about what can happen when a group has an ongoing commitment to dissolving all boundaries.

When we first started working with Roca, we were introduced to a strong and vibrant organization already hiring youth to take on significant roles in the running of the organization, already working in circle and using many principles of collective leadership. They were living what some other groups were only beginning to explore.

For Roca, coming to the KLCC community provided a different kind of opportunity. As Anisha Chablani, one of the leaders of the organization explained, Roca has had a long history of working with youth involved with violence. Through circle, these youth develop the skills and abilities that allow them to be restored to the life of community. The last step in this healing process is for the youth to move from a place of receiving help to one where they are giving back to the community. It is this last step that the KLCC work supported. The fellows involved in KLCC were asked what community issue most stirred their passions. The fellows answered by choosing projects that offered support to immigrants in their community.

Roca is committed to being in circle, even when not in circle. This is a commitment to keeping in mind that each of us is whole, even when our life choices make it hard for us or others to remember that. When we see each other's wholeness, all boundaries dissolve.

This commitment underlies all the work done by Roca, and the fellows' work with the immigrants in their community is no exception. Their outlook has profoundly influenced their take on the question of immigration that our country is trying to address, a question that is all about boundary crossing.

This last story shows what happens when the energy most people use to hold onto boundaries gets used, instead, to enlarge the idea of community. Victor Jose Santana tells this story, in which immigrants are seen not as strangers but rather as neighbors. Victor Jose is a staff person at Roca who works with immigration issues and is a circle keeper. In his story he includes some thoughts on the Community Learning Exchange (CLE) that Roca hosted in Washington, D.C.

This CLE provided an opportunity for immigrants to better understand how democracy works in this country and to help others broaden their thinking about immigration. So often, people focus on the laws about who can come to this country and who can't. This misses the reality of the lives of the many immigrants already here, some who are documented and some who are not; and misses, too, that some of the deported immigrants have children who are U.S. citizens, born on U.S. soil.

....

KNOW YOUR RIGHTS—FIND YOUR POWER
by Victor Jose Santana

Several years ago, ICE (Immigration and Customs Enforcement) agents raided a New Bedford, Massachusetts, leather factory, and arrested three hundred and sixty-one workers, mostly women. Almost immediately, ICE moved to detain and deport most of the workers, eventually moving about two hundred people to facilities in south Texas. This move separated these people—some of whom were parents—from their families and children. It also meant that the workers lost access to a group of pro bono lawyers in Massachusetts.

At Roca we saw how this raid caused widespread fear in the immigrant community. To respond to that fear we formed the Pro-Immigrant Group. This youth and adult partnership organizes around the issue of immigrant rights. The group created a *"Know Your Rights"* booklet that clearly outlines peoples' rights and the steps they can take to keep themselves and their families safe in the event of an immigration raid. To date we have distributed five thousand of these booklets.

We knew that just handing out the booklets was not enough, so we planned to offer workshops where people could get still more information and ask questions. First, the Pro-Immigrant Group got training on how to run the workshops. Another Roca group, the Roca Immigrant and Refugee Initiative (RIRI) provided that training.

Once the training was completed, we put on many workshops. Roxannie DeJesus of RIRI's Coming of Age staff talks about this, "One of our goals was to educate our community on their rights and minimize the fear people were feeling after the New Bedford raids. After one Know Your Rights workshop, a woman came up to me and said, 'Now that I know my rights, I feel safer.' These kinds of comments let us know the workshops are working."

RIRI also offers peacemaking circles to help heal, support, and connect families who have been separated or who are on the verge of being separated due to detention or deportation. This is a very painful time

Collective leadership practitioners from Roca co-hosted a Community Learning Exchange in Washington, D.C., on the impact of immigration reform on youth and families. Photo by Juan Ozuna

when people are picked up and disappear and you don't know what will happen to them. It is a time when we have to support each other to find the strength and courage to keep fighting.

Part of the fight is to take on the issues of policy about how immigrants are treated. RIRI has worked to help shape future Massachusetts immigration policies by engaging very high-risk immigrant young people, community members and leaders, other non-profit organizations, and local government and state agencies in that effort. We feel certain that including the voices of immigrant youth in this process is changing the outcome.

Roca and three other groups have also collected data from a series of public hearings across the state that will affect future immigration policy in Massachusetts.

Most recently, the Community Learning Exchange in Washington, D.C., provided me with an opportunity to share what I have learned about working with immigrant youth and families. This was done in partnership with other groups from around the country committed to the practice of place-based collective leadership.

The three-day event proved to be a powerful one. We began by getting to know each other and sharing stories specific to immigration, ancestry and all the places we had come from. This reminded all of us of the effects of change and movement in communities, countries and families. After that, the CLE opened up for deeper discussions around support, constitutional and civil rights and immigration law.

The design of the CLE allowed us to extend our circle beyond the place where we were meeting. We were able to visit national and local organizations and institutions that serve immigrant communities and work on informing public policy. The combination of these experiences and the learning that came out of them allowed us to come together and create action plans for all the communities we came from.

Often we can feel isolated in our work. Strengthening our connections with other community change agents can be a vital part of renewing energy. Not only did the CLE in Washington, D.C., increase compassion and knowledge around the important issue of immigration, the CLE also provided a safe space for many of us to think critically and to reflect on what we could do to push this movement forward in our respective communities.

The young people and I left the CLE in Washington, D.C., feeling inspired, liberated and full of ideas that we shared with others upon our return.

What we have learned throughout this process is that most people want the same things in life—employment, education, safety, and good health. Many of the country's immigrant youth are facing the challenging dilemma of trying to live in a country that has labeled them as "illegal." It is our hope that we can continue to bring the voice of immigrant youth to the ears of our policy makers. One day we shall stand by the words of Emily Lazarus, written in 1883 at the bottom of our beloved Statue of Liberty:

Give me your tired, your poor,
Your huddled masses yearning to breathe free,
The wretched refuse of your teeming shore.
Send these, the homeless, tempest-tossed to me,
I lift my lamp beside the golden door!

....

CLOSING THOUGHTS

What we know about boundary crossing is that it usually takes us out of our comfort zones. We also know that if we want our communities to be different than they currently are, we must move out of these comfort zones to make something better happen.

One of the critical skills leaders need is to be able to stand in the tension that comes from holding multiple ideas and points of view at the same time. We live in a polarizing time in which people are routinely pushed to pick a position and stay with it, advocating for a particular outcome. Unfortunately, when we go this route, we diminish our resources and the collective power of each community's shared imagination. We limit the possibilities that can only emerge when we are open to learning something new from a person or group that we do not currently know.

It is easy to view those who are different from us as something "less than." We tend to view the melting pot as an invitation to newcomers to give up their identities. In collective leadership, something new and different occurs. In profound new ways, we come to see all of our different identities as a source of vibrant strength, growth, and renewal. When we are willing to cross boundaries and to bring together the many perspectives that exist in a community, we stand a better chance of creating hope as well as healthy communities for ourselves and for all of the members of our community. This hope extends to creating a more compassionate vision for all the communities of our world.

THE Y.A.P. RAP

Lyrics by Adam Roybal & Eric Sotelo

Chorus
I DON'T KNOW WHAT YOU HEARD ABOUT ME
BUT I'M A TEACH YOU 'BOUT THE Y.A.P.s
NO INTERRUPTIN' PEOPLE WHEN WE SPEAK

The fellowship—we're in a meeting
We're working on projects
We got a thing for the city,
The people, the problems

We know that if we work together
Then maybe we'll solve them
So we get youth and adults together
And we get it goin'

We run a peace circle
Just to get to know each other
An hour later, we're all talking
With one another
I love you homie
Hey Man you're like my older brother
You're like the other part of me
Except a little younger

You like the youth, You like adults
You like the way we work
We show respect and always value
Everybody's worth

I'm not that kid trying to holla
Cause I'm acting out
Naw, I'm that kid trying to holla
'Cause I want to help

I'm an adult, but I know what the Y.A.P.s about
Collective Leadership
Not leaving anybody out
Look baby this is simple you can't see
You rollin' with me
You rollin' with that Y.A.P.

Adam Roybal (left) and Eric Sotelo performing their Y.A.P Rap during a presentation at the W.K. Kellogg Foundation. Photo by Cheryl D. Fields

CHAPTER THREE

TRUSTING AND TAPPING INTO COMMUNITY WISDOM

by Dale Nienow
with Elaine Salinas and Graham Hartley

How is collective leadership able to find innovative solutions to old problems?

In this chapter, we explore the third pattern of working together that collective leaders cultivate: **We trust community wisdom and tap into it to find the answers it holds** *by building partnerships based on mutuality.*

When we deeply respect and honor our partnerships, we create a sense of interdependence and security that makes our social fabric more resilient.

In this chapter, Dale explores what is involved in trusting community wisdom and tapping into it. He begins by inviting the reader to rethink the basic assumptions we make about how we can best help our communities, telling stories that illustrate his points. He then offers a case study that describes one community's extensive efforts to develop partnerships of mutuality, which is key to this pattern.

The Editors

P eople get left behind by institutions and systems. That's easy to see in the communities where there is a concentration of poverty, poor nutrition and health, limited educational success, high unemployment, and high incarceration rates. In other communities, it is less visible. We often don't see the people excluded from health care, students dropping out of school, or workers whose jobs have unsafe conditions and pay low wages because those individuals often blend in with the rest of their more prosperous communities.

Of course, many times we don't want to see the downsides of our society as it raises uncomfortable questions. We may not want to acknowledge the shortcomings or consequences of institutions and systems that fail to serve or even harm parts of the community. Some people, because they personally have been well served by those same institutions and systems, may be inclined to say that if others have been harmed, it is probably because those others have made bad choices.

Collective leadership attracts people who are seeking to build a more just and inclusive society. It focuses on changing our shared story to one in which communities, families, and children living on the margins can also benefit from the common good. And, for us, collective leadership has proven so effective in this effort that its principles now underlie all we do to shape community change.

COMMUNITY WISDOM

Each community has its own wisdom, and when a community trusts that wisdom it will discover the unique set of changes community members need to make to help themselves. That assumption is one of the key principles of collective leadership. This call to trust community wisdom has three important aspects: a belief that communities have the wisdom they need to address issues, an understanding of how important it is for communities to claim their own power, and a transformed view of what is helpful to communities that appear to have few resources.

1. What do you believe about community wisdom?

An important premise of collective leadership is that *communities have the wisdom they need* to address local issues. This essential wisdom is often below the surface of what people see. It is the accumulation of knowledge and insights held by a wide range of people from diverse parts of the community, particularly those who have been marginalized and previously left out of leadership.

We have to gather this wisdom in order to improve communities. It is not possible for leaders in institutions and systems to understand all of the perspectives of the community sufficiently to be able to make decisions that benefit the whole community. A story about this:

A small community in the Yukon region of Canada had a disproportionately high incarceration rate of First Nation residents. As with many communities, they were stuck in a cycle that kept the First Nation population from moving forward, which, of course, impedes the larger community as well. The community wanted to transform the justice system to help restore health to the community. Traditionally, any time someone broke a law there was strict enforcement. Once offenders became engaged with the criminal justice system, they tended to return over and over again. Some leaders in the system decided to explore alternative approaches. In trying to figure out how to hold the offender accountable *and* restore the community, the leaders brought together community members not always included in that discussion, including the victim of the crime and the families of the accused person.

When considering what punishment was appropriate for a man accused of theft, they asked these community members to share their perspectives. The accused man's wife said, "If you want to punish my husband, send me to jail. If you send him to jail, he will have his housing, three meals a day, and he will be able to exercise. All these things will be provided for him. If I go to jail, he will have to find a way to feed our kids, get them to school, hold a job, and pay the rent and the bills. He will have to learn to be responsible."

This perspective opens up a different conversation about accountability, rehabilitation, and restoration of community health. Typically, we exclude the perspectives and voices of those who can provide the most useful insights. With its emphasis on trusting community wisdom, collective leadership raises the question, "Who needs to be in the room for us to better understand this issue and to advance our community?"

Believing in community wisdom does not mean that communities do not benefit from resources and ideas from those outside their community. It is clear that economic investment, educational opportunities, and creative programs can be powerful supports to a community. It is critical, however, that these resources and ideas be connected to the local wisdom so they will work and ultimately benefit that community. Another story:

A small manufacturing firm decided to locate a plant in a rural community in Northern Wisconsin. They brought to the community an expertise in manufacturing and how to operate a successful business. They brought a supply of good-paying jobs to the community. In the first year of operation, as fall approached, a majority of employees requested vacation for the week deer hunting season opened. If management approved the request, they would have to greatly curtail production. They knew this was no way to run a business, so they denied the requests and said that anyone who failed to show up for work that week would be fired.

Many of the residents of this community chose to live in the area because of the rich opportunities to be in nature, particularly to hunt and fish. Deer hunting was a family ritual for many. It was an opportunity to bond across generations. It was a way to bring home a year's supply of meat. It also connected to their celebration of Thanksgiving, and the gratitude the community felt for the natural resources they enjoyed. Deer hunting was deeply embedded in the culture.

When hunting season opened, the employees did not go to work; they went hunting. The plant was forced to shut down temporarily and the employees were fired. Eventually, the management rehired most of the employees. The next year, they agreed to let the employees take vacation when hunting season opened. The employees increased productivity before and after the week, leading to a net increase in overall production. They more than made up for their absence from work in that first week of deer season.

It is only when the lens of community wisdom is applied to ideas and resources that come from outside the community that those offerings can be properly adapted to the community's unique circumstances.

2. How do communities view their own power?

With collective leadership, *community groups claim their own power to make positive changes.* Even though people in marginalized communities face daily challenges that can often leave them feeling helpless, some of these communities are tapping into their rich human resources to improve local conditions.

In South Texas, many of the residents are immigrants who have come to the United States to do farm work or to work in factories. Often, they are in low-wage jobs that keep them from affording market-rate housing. As happens in low-income communities, families resort to living in areas with substandard housing. Along the Texas-Mexico border, these areas are called *colonias*, which is defined by the Texas Secretary of State's office as "a residential area lacking some of the most basic living necessities, such as potable water and sewer systems, electricity, paved roads, and safe and sanitary housing."

Colonia has another meaning in Spanish: community. This definition, rather than focusing on deficits, suggests something positive, as community speaks of people coming together to support each other. That is what we experienced in a recent trip to South Texas for a gathering on collective leadership and poverty. We participated in a house meeting in a colonia near San Juan. Rather than being facilitated by a professional community organizer, this meeting was run by a mother of three young children, who lived in the colonia.

She opened the meeting with a prayer, and then asked each of the dozen participants what issues they wanted to address. They decided to focus on the issue of getting the county to install street lights as a safety measure—the lights would reduce both crime and accidents. The group shared strategies for making their case to the county decision-makers. In the room was Teresa Barrera, a woman who had been attending house meetings for thirty-five years. She told of how she and others had been successful in bringing electricity, water, paved streets, and street signs to other colonias in the area. They had also succeeded in connecting with other colonias to bring about state-wide laws to ensure better services.

During her story a big smile came across her face. She said, "They even named a street after me." Having street signs meant that ambulances and fire trucks could find their house in emergencies. She said she had made calling the county commissioners the last thing of her day each day until they responded.

Though we sat among the poorest people of the region, there was not one ounce of helpless resignation in the room. This was a community that believed in themselves and in what was right. Because of this confidence, they were able to draw on the wisdom of the community to bring the key issues to the right leaders in way that improved the lives of the whole community.

3. What kind of help will draw out the assets of the community?

Collective leadership cultivates relationships of mutuality in which *each participant acknowledges and benefits from the gifts of the other.* Sometimes organizations and groups want to help other communities by offering a solution, or by seeking in some way to fix others. This approach assumes something is missing. When we trust community wisdom, we are looking for assets not deficits. It changes how we understand what is helpful.

As Paulo Freire has said, "Authentic help means that all who are involved help each other mutually, growing together in common effort to understand the reality they seek to transform. Only through such praxis—in which those who help and those who are being helped help each other simultaneously—can the act of helping become free from the distortion in which the helper dominates the helped."[2]

La Union del Pueblo Entero (LUPE), a group founded by Cesar Chavez to support farm workers, holds a similar belief. In LUPE's union hall is a banner quoting Lila Watson: "If you have come here to help me, you are wasting your time. But if your liberation is bound up with mine, then let us work together."

---

2 Freire, Paulo. (1978). *Pedagogy in Process: The Letters to Guinea-Bissau.* New York: Continuum

La Union del Pueblo Entero (Lupe) co-hosted a Community Learning Exchange in South Texas on the role collective leadership can play in shaping public policy around poverty issues.
Photo by Dale Nienow

This lens opens up new opportunities for deeper relationship and transformation.

One spring, when dozens of national media descended on a small coal mining community in West Virginia to cover a mining disaster, they were expecting limited access to resources such as restaurants. Over the course of the week, an abundant buffet of food appeared. It was cooked by residents and donated by businesses in the community. Associated Press Editor Peter Prengaman reported, "Imagine, here we are, an aggressive and hard-charging bunch of journalists in the middle of this devastated community, and it's THEY who are taking care of US!" In the midst of great poverty and community disaster, and counter to the common stereotype, these West Virginians were teaching the world about generosity.

In any community, there are many gifts we will see if we will open our eyes to respectful relationships and see without judgment or condescension. From our experiences in Appalachia, we would add to generosity, the gifts of hospitality, loyalty, hard work, resilience, and faith. They have much to teach us as we work together.

TAPPING INTO COMMUNITY WISDOM

Believing in the importance of local wisdom is one aspect of collective leadership; tapping into that wisdom is another. Drawing out the collective wisdom of the community is not an automatic occurrence. It requires establishing trust and opening hearts through compassion. It can flow more readily when partnerships have been established based on mutuality rather than on a hierarchy of power, or a one-way relationship.

Some people and communities have been so poorly treated that they have built up barriers of self protection in order to survive. When some-one has been marginalized or continually experienced disparities as the result of institutional and system practices, his/her mistrust of others is an essential strategy to navigate daily life. When people have been left behind in their communities, they will not easily establish the relationships that enable community members to share wisdom freely. Trust cannot be assumed. Belief in the good intentions of others cannot be taken for granted. When seeking to engage community members in change work, if we want to open avenues for trust to emerge, we must first behave in ways that prove trustworthiness. This is particularly true when one party holds more power or resources than the other. All parties need to be clear that building the relationship will lead to a shared goal of long term mutual well being and community health. Asking for someone's contribu-tion without first establishing long-term engagement will limit how much community wisdom gets shared.

Individuals who hold certain positions or resources often expect to direct change initiatives or to manage community institutions. It is often a shift for these individuals who are used to wielding influence to "hold their power lightly" so that the voices of other community members and organizations can be fully heard and respected. When these positional leaders create space for authentic partnerships, it is more likely that com-munity members will be willing to take the risk to open up and share their gifts and perspectives. This shift from a desire to direct/be directed to a desire to collaborate is essential and profound. There is a guide in the Resources section on developing and maintaining mutual partner-ships. It offers ways to initiate this kind of relationship, as well as some ideas on how to handle the practical challenges of working together in this non-hierarchal way.

People who have experienced the pain and trauma of being invisible or treated as "less than" do not always feel that their voice and contribu-tions are valued. They may need space and time for healing or for others to witness and affirm their stories and experiences. This often requires creating spaces, such as Gracious Space and circle, where people can hold themselves and each other with compassion.

As people in community begin to experience compassion, it can open their hearts to new relationships. They may open up in awkward ways, initially making statements that push others back. At these times, compassionate listening rather than giving back a harsh statement is usually the most helpful response. This is not an easy process.

We hosted a community gathering once with the children of survivors of the killing fields of the Pol Pot regime in Cambodia. These were young college students from Cambodia who were in the United States to learn professional skills to help heal their country. They told of how their parents' generation had experienced so much trauma that they did not know how to parent or shape the development of young people. In this discussion was a resident of the U.S., Saroeum Phoung, who had emigrated from Cambodia, having escaped the Pol Pot regime. He had learned the process of peacemaking circles while working with gangs and pursuing restorative justice in his Chelsea, Massachusetts community. He had learned how to deal with his own pain.

The students had rarely been in the presence of a healthy Cambodian adult role model. Saroeum offered them the following exercise. He asked for a volunteer to stand up and hold his arm straight out while holding a full bottle of water. After about five minutes, he asked the volunteer how his arm felt. The volunteer replied that it was starting to ache. "Imagine holding the bottle for a day, or a week. Now imagine what holding in pain does to us if the pain has been in us for a year, or a lifetime."

Pain of any magnitude distorts us. We need to let it out in ways that will transform us to health. To do this requires great compassion—standing with each other with love rather than pity or judgment. When we do this, people will heal, groups will heal and then they will be able to share their gifts. This will open up the great resource of our communities' essential wisdom.

PUTTING COMMUNITY WISDOM INTO ACTION IN MINNEAPOLIS

The following story shows how community wisdom can be accessed through the practice of collective leadership, and how this approach has fostered sustainable change in one community. The story highlights MIGIZI Communication, Inc., a community-based organization serving Native Americans in Minnesota's Twin Cities. MIGIZI is one of a group of organizations that have worked the last eight years to ensure that all students in the Minneapolis school system have equal opportunities to learn. As these groups have joined efforts to pursue educational equity, they have developed into a close-knit, cross-cultural collaborative.

Minnesota has long held a reputation for high quality public education.

Nationally, their high school graduation rates have been near the top, and a high percentage of the people in the Minneapolis and St. Paul metropolitan area have college degrees. Yet over the past three decades, the demographics of the Minneapolis public schools have changed dramatically.

The Twin Cities have become a major center for refugees with large populations of Hmong and Somalis. As with much of the rest of the country, the Latino population has also increased. These groups have joined the African Americans and Native Americans already in the community. At the same time, more of the white population has moved to suburban school districts or enrolled their children in independent schools.

Schools may have worked well for whites, but not so well for Native Americans, recent immigrants, refugees, and other communities of color. When data on school success was aggregated, results looked good. When the data was disaggregated, it revealed experiences that varied widely among different groups. For instance, the Native American graduation rate was 18 percent compared to 84 percent for whites.

The disaggregated data supports what Elaine Salinas, president of MIGIZI Communications, has to say about the typical approach schools take. She says, "They have a one-size-fits-all mentality. They focus on things that will apply to the greatest numbers of kids. If you're culturally distinct, it's hard to fit into that mold. The system has never worked for our kids."

In The Beginning—Challenging First Steps

Elaine Salinas, and her colleague Graham Hartley, director of programs at MIGIZI, met with us to reflect on the work their organization and other groups are doing to help all students in the Minneapolis school system to reach their potential.

Eight years ago, MIGIZI was selected to be part of the Kellogg Foundation's Leadership for Community Change (KLCC) initiative that was to focus on ways to improve teaching and learning. Kellogg invited MIGIZI and other groups to cross boundaries of race and culture so they could cultivate collective leadership and jointly improve their community. MIGIZI worked to bring together the African American, African immigrant, Latino, Hmong, and Native American communities. The hope was that these five different cultural communities would form a fellowship that could interact with the schools in a way that would help all students of color.

MIGIZI had previously worked with organizations from different cultural

Elaine Salinas, executive director of MIGIZI Communications in Minneapolis, Minnesota.
Photo by Cheryl D. Fields

communities on a community technology project. In the KLCC initiative, however, MIGIZI reached deeper into these communities and engaged emerging leaders rather than the official representatives of organizations they had worked with earlier. The first conversations about improving education and learning were challenging. Not all the participants were ready to focus on the educational issues they had in common across the cultural communities. Some felt that having MIGIZI —or any agency that was already committed to a particular cultural community—as the lead agency, would mean a loss of power for their own group.

Looking back, Elaine talks about the lesson learned, "How you position yourself when you are working with diversity is important. MIGIZI was established as the lead KLCC agency in the Twin Cities. The history of cultural communities is they have had to compete with each other for attention, for resources, for everything. It is problematic for an Indian organization to lead an African American organization. Even though we were dealing with individuals, this perspective still carried over. There are internal tensions that we are always trying to work through."

Adapting The Approach

It was clear that there was concern that the specific issues of each cultural community would get lost if the groups moved too quickly to develop a common vision and strategy. Because little time had been spent on building relationships with each other, trust was also an issue. They decided to adapt their original plan by dividing into separate cultural groups. Each group would then fashion their own agenda for working with the schools. Breaking into groups allowed each group to tap into their own community's wisdom and to use it to shape how they approached the schools.

During this phase, the connections between groups were loosely held. Some of the groups—the Hmong, Latino, and Native American groups—shared more regularly with each other. The African American group spun off into parallel efforts with less frequent contact.

"It appeared like we were faltering regarding collective leadership because the work was more hands off," Graham explains. "But it was good, because we put the responsibility for the work in the hands of the community, we let them do the work. Some powerful initiatives emerged from each group.

"Two brothers were instrumental in starting a Hmong academy here in Minneapolis. It is a contract with Minneapolis public schools, and incorporates their culture and language into the operation of the school."

Elaine adds, "The Latino group was working with youth. The African American community was doing spoken word, hip hop, anti-violence with youth and they are still doing that today."

During this time when groups were focusing on their own communities' needs, the Native American community worked to forge a new relationship between their community and the school district. They directed the schools' attention to how Native Americans have experienced education in the past, and how that experience affects families' decisions today.

Native Americans have had a long history of education being used as a tool to stamp out their language and culture. The boarding school movement alienated many Native Americans from their own culture. What little of the Native American story that has made it into the curriculum is mostly negative. It is understandable that even today when Native American children struggle in school or experience conflict of some kind, the family may not insist that the student stay in school. Families have learned not to trust the system.

MIGIZI has helped lead the effort to get the Native American community involved in their youth's success in school. One major result is that a landmark Memorandum of Agreement (MOA) between the Native American community and the Minneapolis school board now governs how the schools work with Native American students and families.

"What the MOA has done for us," Elaine says, "is to provide leverage to move the bar. We have been able to say that Indian students are not invisible, and that even though we are the smallest subgroup, you have to pay attention. It has brought the community into direct conversations with the school board, which never happened before."

Opening The Door Wider

With this new relationship with the school district in place, the Native American community has been able to bring their community wisdom into the schools in a number of ways. "We are becoming part of the district-wide professional staff development schedule," Elaine points out. "This is one of the things we wanted to be able to do—to train teachers. We developed a curriculum for teachers to help them develop an understanding of the Dakota history as the original people of the Minneapolis area."

Graham adds, "What that does for the teachers is it really gets them to look at Native kids in their classroom in a different light—where there is a greater, a deeper sense of respect and acknowledgment. I think it is a really valuable thing for teachers to be respectful of their kids. We talk about educators commanding the respect of their students, but it is a two-way street."

There are two Native American staff who now work in the schools as a result of the MOA. They not only help teachers develop culturally sound curriculum, but also guide them in their relationships with students and families.

"Their focus right now is on trying to educate the parents; to empower them to be more active and advocate for their children," Elaine says.

MIGIZI also helped the Native American community organize to elect the first Native American to the public school board.

Coming Full Circle—What Is Partnership?

As the various cultural communities made progress on their educational agendas, they stayed connected enough to share their lessons and to build deeper relationships. This interaction ultimately led to organizing a new coalition called the Educational Equity Organizing Collaborative (EEOC). The initial coalition, which has since expanded, included MIGIZI, the Somali Action Alliance, the Latino arm of ISAIAH (a faith-based alliance), and the Organizing Apprenticeship Project. The EEOC brings a collective voice to the school district. It is the cross boundary approach to leadership originally envisioned eight years ago with an important difference.

In Elaine's words, "We decided as a collaborative that there was no leader, we were all partners. When we formed the EEOC, we decided not to go in with a set agenda. We were all interested in education—the schools were failing all our kids. And so we knew each community would have its own agenda, and that there would also be a cross cutting agenda we could share—but we agreed that we would support each other in our individual agendas. I think that was very important."

The EEOC has been a channel for conversations between the communities and the school board and administrators.

"The school board came to us and asked if we would organize our groups in support of a school funding referendum," Elaine recalls. "Because we were the gateway into cultural communities, they realized they needed to work with us because the referendum would not pass without the cultural communities.

"We wanted people to understand that we were going to vote for the referendum, but, if it passed, it would be followed by some demands for accountability. The referendum was necessary, but not sufficient to help Native American children. The referendum passed by the biggest margin that a referendum had ever passed. And the superintendent, the next day, called the EEOC and thanked us. And now we are working on holding the school board accountable. That's why we have had these follow-up sessions that the school board and administration agreed to—with the EEOC, parents, and the board."

Elaine admits there have also been moments of disappointment when the school district has not followed through on commitments.

Collective leadership fellows in Minneapolis, Minnesota. Photo by John Guthrie

"We had a defining moment a couple of years ago. The school was going to hire a new Indian education director. Everything to do with Indian education came to a standstill. Then they ended up hiring someone who had no experience with the MOA. So we were really upset. We talked about how we were going to respond. In the past, we would have ranted and raved. This time we went to the school board and they didn't know what to expect. We got up and told them how difficult it was to be part of this partnership, especially when one partner doesn't follow through on what they agreed to do. But instead of ranting and raving, we invited them to dinner to have a conversation.

"So we had dinner with them. We had a conversation about partnership and what it means for the school board member and what it means from the Indian perspective. One of the school members said—and I will remember this forever—'What partnership means to me is that each partner feels they have the ability to influence the other partners.' It hit home to me because that is something the Indian community never feels. We can't influence this partnership as much as we want to—but we have a lot more influence than we ever had before."

Trust is building. The school board now knows that when they are invited to show up in community, there will not automatically be an attack on them, but more likely the meeting will be an opportunity to develop the partnership. The shift from confrontation to collaboration is opening up more possibilities. Throughout all the changes and obstacles, the community has been able to provide a stable voice—they have had the staying power needed to continue progress. And each transition in school board membership tests the strength of the agreement with the community.

The Work Continues

In reflecting on how the EEOC has developed, Elaine remarks, "We work closely in that collaborative. I love that collaborative because we all get along, we respect each other. It really is a partnership. And now we have brought in four new organizations because we are becoming statewide.

"Here is our next work. A couple of years ago, our governor was going to give funding to schools making the greatest progress under No Child Left Behind. He called it the Star Schools Project. The money was to go to schools that were scoring the highest on tests. There was a huge outcry because it would have meant that the suburban schools that are already doing well would have got the most money—not the inner city schools that most need the resources—and he was never able to implement it.

"So our idea is this. We want to create a process, and potentially lobby into state law, a recognition of schools that are models of racially equitable education. We are going to be developing the rubric for what that would look like. The rubric will address broad categories—we are just starting to outline it—student performance, the school environment, the composition of the teaching force—all these different things. We will look at all these things in building a definition of what a racially and culturally equitable school looks like.

"And then to reward them, to recognize them, we want a state incentive system. We want this to be statewide. What we are trying to do is to push the bar. We want people to talk about not just test scores, but beyond test scores. To get people thinking about what is a good education. What does it really entail? And test scores are part of that—or academic achievement. But it is just a part of it. There are all these other pieces that are equally important.

"Public schools used to be about teaching people to be good citizens. That was the fundamental purpose. But look how far we have gotten away from that.

"I am really excited about this piece! Our plan is to take people over to the state capitol in droves. Whenever we show up with groups of people of color, you almost close everything down. If you walk into a hearing with a group of people of color, everything stops.

"To me the EEOC is the next generation. It is the work that was started with the collective leadership of KLCC. It has led us here."

The Work Shared

The story of Minneapolis cannot end without mentioning MIGIZI's involvement in a learning community called the Community Learning Exchange (CLE), which has allowed them to link with other communities across the nation that are also working on teaching and learning issues. Communities share their successful approaches to leadership and change with each other. MIGIZI has hosted a learning exchange on educational equity with another community organization from Wisconsin, New Paradigm Partners.

As communities send their local partners to national gatherings, the attendees can get out of their local routines, reflect on their work together, strengthen relationships, and open up to new ideas emerging from other communities. It allows hosting organizations to deepen their local partnerships, and to see how connected their change work is to that of other communities across the country.

Elaine offers this: "In the CLE meetings, we are focused on the work.

Photo courtesy of Big Creek People in Action

We need to understand each other, and the learning exchange helps us get to know our partners better. Two of our upcoming leaders were so encouraged by the gathering they attended, they are now more vocal in meetings. They have come to see their work as part of a larger movement."

People doing the hard work of making change in challenging environments need a way to inspire and support each other as they learn together and plan together. The time taken to reflect upon and evaluate their efforts makes them more adaptive and better able to respond to issues and opportunities. Learning communities are not a luxury, but a fundamental social change strategy. They help sustain the passion of the group and keep them open to transformation.

Hosting a learning exchange allowed MIGIZI and its partners an opportunity to share rich stories of culture and history of place, build trust through Gracious Space and other collective leadership processes, and engage participants in experiential activities they could use in their home communities.

CLOSING THOUGHTS

Finding a way for the essential wisdom of each cultural community to surface and to form the basis of strategies to work with the schools is paying off in the Minneapolis school system. It has deepened each group's confidence to work with other groups, and has extended the building of trusting relationships. Because these groups have created more trust with each other and with the schools, they can have more honest conversation. For Native American students, the high school graduation rate has almost tripled in the past decade.

The trusting relationships have taken time and effort to develop. In that process, these diverse groups have come to realize that they can, in fact, act together in ways that are mutually beneficial, ways that have made each group, as well as the community as a whole, stronger.

The Minneapolis story is one of many demonstrating that collective leadership is emerging as a prominent force—or movement—for our time. Because it is based on the premise that both the needed leadership and the needed answers will emerge from the collective wisdom of the group, it works well across many cultures. It helps to improve the day-to-day realities of people who have been left out of societal benefits—people of color, women, youth, low-income—and it does this is by engaging them *in* leadership. Because collective leadership is so inclusive, the wisdom of diverse perspectives in the community can be honored. It offers a hopeful way to engage the mix of cultures present in most communities in this country. As Elaine Salinas says, "When the community's wisdom can lead the process, fundamentally the community realizes its power. We know we have power."

SEEDS
by Robert "Bob" Tenequer

In a basket: our mother brought us seeds of corn.
Nestled in her palm were seeds of different colors:
red, white, yellow & blue.
Which one is you?
To the seeds in her open hand she shared her wisdom,
knowledge, respect, courage and generosity.
She then sprinkled corn pollen on each seed as they
were planted in the soft earth.
She called on the rain clouds
She then welcomed the sun
As the sun rose, Kokopelli played his flute
As the plants grew the drums began to beat to announce
the birth of a new nation.

KLCC Fellowship, Eastern Cibola County, New Mexico. Photo by Randy Siner

CHAPTER FOUR

CULTIVATING STORIES OF CHANGE

by Francisco Guajardo and Miguel Guajardo

How does collective leadership open a path to a better future for ourselves, our organizations, and our communities?

In this chapter, we explore the fourth pattern of working together that collective leaders cultivate: **We know our story and together imagine the narrative for our community.** *This allows us to reframe the present and direct our actions towards a good future.*

Using our imagination to weave our stories into the social fabric gives us direction over our lives and a sense of legitimacy. The cloth becomes strong and one that holds us all.

In this chapter, Francisco and Miguel explore how telling our stories is key to identity formation. They show how stories are data that, when analyzed, can lead to creating strategies for change. This approach opens up imagination and creativity.

The Editors

THE FIELD

A few years ago, Reynaldo, a student in a rural south Texas high school, used acrylic paint to draw an image on thin masonite board. He drew and painted the piece as part of a place-based arts project sponsored by the Llano Grande Center, a nonprofit education organization, and he was inspired by an art teacher's challenge to reflect on his family narrative. His response to that challenge was what he calls "La Labor," or "The Field." For Reynaldo, the painting has meaning beyond the literal piece of land lined with seemingly unending rows of crops. In his painting, he captures the experience and history of his family life, one defined by seasonal migrant farm labor in different parts of the country. "My family has been shaped by the experience of the field," Reynaldo has said, explaining the broader meaning of his art. "It's about the struggle, about the lessons, and about the stories. It's about what we have learned."

"The Field" is also about how we envision a better world, how we look forward, as we reflect back. Reynaldo is a practitioner in the leadership for community change movement in his region, and he views the "field" as the expansive ground from which we take the greatest lessons. In this way, he has taken the image of the field and turned it into a metaphor—the field as the laboratory for learning, just as it is also the archive of lessons from the past.

"La Labor" by Reynaldo Garcia

Reynaldo's story is captivating, through its visual aesthetic, and in its narrative form. And, as often happens when one starts to tell one's own story—whether it be through words or painting—Reynaldo began to understand better who he was. It is one of story's gifts that when a person or a group tells a story about themselves, they to begin to develop a clearer identity of who they are.

In Reynaldo's story of "The Field," we see, too, the compelling power of story to replace old narratives and create counter narratives to support new directions for community. "The figure is looking toward the horizon," said Reynaldo, "because he can imagine something better."

Good stories capture the imagination. There is a part of the brain, argue cognitive psychologists, that privileges stories. Human beings tend to pay attention more when one utters the words, "Let me tell you a story." We hear it from the most effective teachers, from parents who understand how to get through to their children, from the successful salespeople. The story form is a useful method for teaching and learning; it is a useful method for raising children; and it's a useful method for organizing people and communities for change.

WHAT OUR PARENTS TAUGHT US

Our parents used stories unabashedly. They remembered things from their childhood and told stories about them. They created new stories to teach values, lessons on life, or simply to motivate their children to do things. We have learned a great deal from our parents, who were both active anthropologists in a Gramscian kind of way—they have always been organic intellectuals, storytellers, and ethnographers.[3] Our parents did not attain formal schooling past their elementary years in rural Mexico. They were, however, curious participants in life, and their curiosity and imagination were parlayed into a continuous generation of stories. They used stories to their advantage, as they raised four boys and managed a household.

So we learned the art of storytelling from our parents, and today their lesson informs our work as parents, teachers, learners, and community developers. It has also become the vehicle for our work as researchers and public educators. Our parents also taught us that stories were inseparable from the art of conversation. Knowing how to have a conversation—understanding how to listen, how to ask questions, how to build on what others say—was a key skill set for the storyteller. The ability to have a meaningful conversation was almost a prerequisite to telling a good story,

---

3 Joll, James. (1977). *Antonio Gramsci.* New York: Viking Press

according to our parents, but before anyone could engage in a meaningful conversation, there were conditions that had to be nurtured.

The necessary conditions our parents spoke about and modeled were akin to Gracious Space, as that concept is elaborated in this book. The conditions bear a striking resemblance to the spirit of circle, as it is used by Roca and discussed in Chapter 2; the circle process has been integral to many organizations' efforts at collective leadership, and has been important to the emerging work of the Community Learning Exchange (CLE). As our parents would have it, the space had to be safe—from violence, from ridicule, from disrespect. The space respected children, just as it demanded that elders be honored. And the space encouraged creativity in all forms.

FIELD WORK

Story is at its best when it is shared, when it becomes public, and when owned by the group. We invite the reader to take an empty seat, to join us in action by sharing and contributing to the story circle. The reader's contribution would expand the conversation and knowledge base in this chapter. Throughout the chapter, we attempt to model shared storytelling by engaging in a conversation, and by expanding the content of our story to include our partners, the creators/artists, performers, and contributors of these stories. To frame our own story in public creates a dynamic of

Story of early formation of selves: field work in a different setting. Photo by Juan Ozuna

dialogue that adds texture, energy, complexity, and power to the storytelling process. It also parallels the collective leadership process we delve into in other chapters of this same book. In isolation, leadership has some utility, but in the collective it provides a radically different view to the story and the imagination we create, including the ability to imagine what is possible. We invite the reader to engage in the crafting of stories and encourage others to co-construct a collective story as part of the quest for teaching, learning and leading.

Stories have been invaluable in our work as teachers, learners, and community builders. It has allowed us to put a face to a place, ground values and history in context, and has assisted in the construction of an identity of people and community. The story has provided oxygen to places and spaces that have historically been unable to breathe in a metaphorical sense because of the forces of economic and other historical marginalization. It has given voice to people who previously have not been part of the public discourse on how we can best teach, learn and lead.

Through story, we construct a new covenant with people, institutions, and communities that search for a better world for themselves and for their children. Stories allow us to dream together, grow together, trust each other, and in solidarity create different stories that give us hope. The relationship that is nurtured in this process also begins to create a field of trust where adults, children, and strangers alike can walk into a space and feel safe to share their story; in short, these relationships allow us to take risks and cross our comfort boundaries in a public setting.

LIFE AS TEXT: A STORY CREATION PROCESS

When we were in elementary school, a few years after having emigrated from Mexico, our family became part of the migrant labor stream. One year we migrated to Buttonwillow, California, where the family hoed weeds most of the summer; another summer we traveled to the Texas Panhandle, where we picked onions; other summers we simply worked the fields in and around our hometown of Elsa in the Rio Grande Valley of south Texas; but the most formative summer was the one we spent in the labor camp in Keeler, a rural community in southwestern Michigan. In Keeler, some of our collective leadership skills began to take shape.

Two interesting stories emerged from our time in Keeler, particularly from a child development and even leadership formation perspective. Because we left south Texas sometime in early April, almost two months before the school year closed, we were obligated to enroll in a local school in Michigan. And we did, in a school in Sister Lakes, a charming coastal

The Guajardo brothers (l-r: Juan Jose "Pepe," Miguel Angel, Francisco Javier and Luis Lauro) outside the housing projects where we grew up. Photo courtesy of the Guajardo family

town by Lake Michigan. One story emerges from that schooling experience. The other comes from evening social activity at the labor camp.

Frequently in the evenings, the four Guajardo boys sat around in a circle outside our cabin at the labor camp, often with other children who lived in neighboring cabins. There, we told stories. Our parents and other adults typically refereed the social activity, ensuring that things were in order, and mostly nurturing the conditions so the kids could engage in a safe and even creative social activity. On many nights, we listened to the radio broadcasts of the Cincinnati Reds baseball games. The Reds were the biggest show in professional sports during those days, the mid-1970s when Pete Rose, Joe Morgan, Johnny Bench, and others formed the core of the "Big Red Machine," the most feared baseball club of the era. Southwestern Michigan was in the neighborhood, so our transistor radio received the Reds' airwaves on most clear summer nights, and the games provided prime material for great theater at the labor camp.

Our brother Juan Jose, "Pepe" we call him, typically played the lead role, as he mimicked Tom Brenneman, the Reds' play-by-play announcer, and one of the younger kids usually performed the color commentating, a la Joe Nuxhall, Brenneman's on-air sidekick. Pepe was the skilled play-by-play man of the family, having honed his skills when he was five, six, and seven, as we listened to the Broncos de Reynosa baseball games on Mexican radio when we lived south of the border. Pepe was quite the performer, using voice inflection, building up drama, and providing thick description of players and their nuances. Some of it he learned from the radio announcers, some he simply made up.

The learning was rich, about baseball, but also about math, as we learned how to calculate batting averages, earned run averages, and such; if Pete Rose got one hit in three at bats, we knew he batted .333 that night. We learned about geography—when manager Sparky Anderson pulled his starting pitcher in the seventh inning and brought in relief pitcher Pedro Borbon from the bullpen, Brenneman was sure to note that Borbon hailed from the Dominican Republic (DR), so we knew where the DR was, just as we knew about Oakland, because Joe Morgan came from there, and so on. As importantly, we learned about language, mainly about usage of the English language, as we listened to Brenneman and Nuxhall; we learned how to pronounce words, learned syntax, and learned certain rhetorical devices, as baseball broadcasting is rich with creative wordsmithing.

And almost nightly at the labor camp, we also learned how to perform. If a game was on that night, Pepe would lead the performance by repeating much of what the announcers said. During commercial breaks, he would create, just as the rest of us would imagine and enunciate scenarios as we provided color commentary to Pepe's play-by-play narration. If the Reds had a night off, then it became pure original theater, as Pepe and his announcing crew created new baseball situations; the action tended to be detailed and intense on these occasions. On those nights, the Reds always won. And so did we.

Our parents and other adults from the labor camp were the producers of this theater, as they ensured that things were safe as we played the games, as the kids collectively created and imagined new plays, and new games. Our parents nurtured the conditions where we could learn the skills, where we could practice our leadership functions, and where we could do it together. This became our rich training ground for group leadership.

During the day, we went to school in Sister Lakes. A yellow school bus stopped outside the camp every morning to pick us up, the migrant kids. Our memory tells us that just about every one of the migrant kids was Mexican or Mexican American, with the possible exception of two kids, who may have been poor whites. The bus then took us to the school in Sister Lakes, where the migrant kids got off the bus and walked to a side door of the schoolhouse that led us to the migrant classroom, in the basement. All the migrant kids went into the basement, and we typically stayed in that room the entire day, except for lunchtime, the only time when migrant students saw the first floor of the school. The migrant classroom included students of all grade levels. First-graders joined second-, third-, and even eighth-graders in that basement classroom. Altogether, more than 40 migrant students filled the crowded basement classroom that was led by a teacher and a teacher's aide.

The teachers were very nice. They seemed to care and showed kindness and sensitivity to the students. The classroom rules were fairly standard, the teaching and learning process typically followed the teaching practices that Martin Haberman has come to call "a pedagogy of poverty," where students sit in rows, listen passively to the teacher, and are asked to memorize facts and then regurgitate them in a test. That was the mode of operation in the migrant classroom.[4]

But most importantly, it was in the basement. That's the lingering memory—that the migrant kids went to school in the basement. We did not mix with the other students, the locals who were not part of the migrant experience. Their classrooms were on the first and second floors, and we rarely saw them, except for glimpses as we came into the schoolhouse in the morning and as we left in the afternoon. It was clear enough to us then that we were treated differently, perhaps even in a manner consistent with segregationist practices. It is difficult to measure the impact of this reality, though we know that a preponderance of evidence suggests that segregationist practices in schools have deep psychological effects on children. The legal and social discourse that surrounded the historic 1954 *Brown v. Board of Education* Supreme Court case elevated into the public consciousness the argument that segregation and its practices adversely affect the psychology of children, and we believe that sending migrant students to the basement constituted a practice of segregation in this particular school. This schooling experience was tantamount to the experience that other children in parts of the Jim Crow south experienced in schools and even in social life. The migrant student experience in southwestern Michigan was very similar. In the mid-1970s, our schooling experience exposed us to the underbelly of our enlightened society. We would have been in serious trouble, if this had been the extent of our educational life.

Fortunately, our educational experience had greater range, because after school the bus took us back to the labor camp, where we prepared for a richer, deeper learning process around storytelling. The Cincinnati Reds

---

4 Haberman, Martin. (1991). "The Pedagogy of Poverty Versus Good Teaching." *Phi Delta Kappan, 73*(4), pg. 290-294

games on the radio offered one excuse around which to convene "class." But even when the Reds were not on the radio, on the off nights, that was when Pepe and the labor camp kids were most "on." Those nights, Pepe created his own play-by-play, others provided color commentary, and we generally told stories. In those creative scenarios that our parents and other adults nurtured, the conditions were clear: egalitarian impulses were encouraged, participation was expected, and we all exercised leadership in a collective way. This was the other emergent story, the one apart from the basement experience.

Discussion of story. Photo by Juan Ozuna

HARVESTING THE STORY

The literature on the use of story is voluminous. Much attention is paid to story as an instrument for narrative inquiry. Studs Terkel explored the broader narrative of America by asking people to tell their stories about living on a street in Chicago. Terkel's storytellers told about life during the Great Depression and shared their truths about their hardscrabble lives and their work. Using fictitious stories, Mark Twain critiqued the life of the ante-bellum American South. Many others use story to celebrate, commemorate, romanticize, or struggle with issues of the past, present, and future. Story is also commonly used as method for analysis, as can be seen in this chapter. We find deep utility in story as a tool for change, in much the same way that Myles Horton, founder of the famed Highlander Folk School (now Highlander Research and Education Center), used it.

As part of our brand of education and training in our south Texas context, we employ Horton's method of tapping into people's stories for the purpose of organizing and implementing social action and educational campaigns. Like Horton, the Llano Grande Center is firm in the belief that stories people and communities carry with them are appropriate and often powerful texts around which curriculum and strategy can be developed. Our use of stories in this chapter is no different from what may transpire in a high school classroom, in a graduate seminar, or in a community campaign. As important, we need school and community leaders to model the act of storytelling, because leaders transfer the skill set from a personal and private process to a public skill set and capacity to act for the public good.

In Horton's autobiography, *The Long Haul*, he characterizes story as a process that moves organically and in stages.[5] He describes a three-stage process in the following way:

1) tell stories to set the context, develop the characters, and build the ideas;
2) ask questions about the story, and exercise the critical eye/"I"; and
3) build an action that grows out of the storytelling process.

Though Horton did not use the metaphor of anatomy to frame the concept of storytelling, we find anatomy an appropriate metaphor through which to make sense of telling stories, asking questions about stories, and developing action plans that respond to the lessons of stories.

THE ANATOMY OF STORY

We view story as a complex and organic process that is at the core of human activity. It is also a highly skilled process. These skills include the understanding of social context. Story is a product of human agency and formation informed by cultural dynamics, local ecology, and history. These different components are molded though a process that filters data, organizes it, and puts it back out in a medium that makes sense. Using the anatomy metaphor, story then flows with a certain rhythm and balance through the following parts:

Navel

Just as the umbilical cord feeds human life during its embryonic stages, we see the navel representing the core of the human anatomy, and as the central component that feeds and balances the story. In storytelling, a balance must be achieved between the message and the core values within the story. The core message and the questions that emerge from the story are elements that spring from the navel and are essential for developing the core purpose of the story.

---

5 Horton, Myles. (1999). *The Long Haul.* New York: Teachers College Press

Heart

The human heart gives the body ultimate meaning, and is the source of human passion; in the same way, the heart of the story is typically its meaning, and even its passionate quality. The passion is shaped by the values that guide the efforts that fuel action. These values include the emotional, moral, and relational ways of knowing the story.

Mind

The mind is the center of all analytical thinking, and at this stage of story development we bring critical analysis to its formation. The mind is what fuels the ideas, the imagination, and instructional action.

Hands

The hands massage and help mold the values, ideas, message, and rhythm of the story. This negotiation of the message is a complex and sophisticated process, and it accounts for environment and tone of the delivery. This is the stage where the story is told and retold until the choice of language, the nonverbal element, and the message are all coordinated and delivered.

Legs

If a story has longevity, if it impacts others beyond the storyteller, it probably has legs. A story with legs is one that lives and moves, could be passed down from generation to generation, and may just stand the test of time. The story with legs also begins to contribute to the identity of place, people, and organizations. The story with legs moves people to action, provokes new questions, and helps identify the work that is connected to the story. Stories with legs also help individuals and groups develop the necessary agency to push, resist and amalgamate the outside forces to allow for the creation of a new reality for the self, the group, and the community in which we live.

We offer this metaphor of the human anatomy as a concrete visual to the abstract concept of story. We firmly believe that everyone can become a storyteller, and we humbly offer this process as a tool for expanding the reader's imagination while also putting forth the ideas that stories are living constructs and are malleable constructions of humans and our environment. In the Resources section you will find a short Guide to Harvesting and Sharing Stories which features a detailed version of this process to help others bring their own stories to life.

A PROCESS FOR IDENTITY FORMATION

Story comes in different forms: narrative, pictures, and performance are a few we write about in this chapter, but clearly there are many more. We see story as a vehicle for placing teaching, learning, and leading into the hands of ordinary people. Without the power of story, Reynaldo would not have voice to share his family's story of struggle and identity formation in the fields. Without the power of story, we would not have had the ability to imagine a world beyond the basement in that elementary school in Michigan; we could not have traveled the world and sat on the front row of the Cincinnati Reds' games while living in the labor camps. Because of the power of story, everything becomes possible. We use story as a process for identity formation, as well as for giving voice to many who do not have the privileges of the traditional forms of power, including the mainstream media, money, and formal educational institutions.

A PROCESS FOR BUILDING RELATIONSHIPS

Humans have been storytellers since time immemorial. The range of story expression can be seen drawn on the inside of ancient caves, acted out in the public square, shared in books, or these days, told through digital media. Regardless of its form, all stories offer a glimpse into people's lives and souls during a particular time in history. Children on the playground share stories with each other. Political candidates on campaign trails share their history, values, and wishes so they can get elected. The story continues to be a key vehicle for building relationship and understanding the values of individuals and groups. When stories are authentic and successful, they are powerful relationship-building tools. On the other hand, when storytelling is successfully used to deceive people, it is a most dangerous tool. Not all stories are noble and not all stories are honest. What is certain is that great power lies with the storyteller; with that comes great responsibility. Storytelling requires a critical eye/I on both the telling and listening sides. We must always be aware of the context, the purpose for the story and the relationships that need to be nurtured to give currency to the story.

CROSSING BOUNDARIES

In our context, as in that of many marginalized (geographically, culturally, and economically) communities, we code switch when we are in conversation, depending on audience. It is especially the case when telling stories. When sharing our stories with the world, we often feel compelled to explain the cultural use of language, nuance, and performance. When we fail to do that, stories may be misinterpreted, or considered ill informed or troublesome. This is one side of the story-telling process. Another is to consider the audience's readiness for the story. What is the audience's level of readiness to understand the story, the willingness to be open to new realities? Is the audience ready to cross boundaries with the storyteller? As the storyteller considers these questions, there is also the issue of one's commitment to the integrity of the story: commitment to the context, to the meaning, and to the impact of the story. Storytelling can be a powerful tool for crossing boundaries of race, class, gender; but it also is essential to establish the Gracious Space conditions of respect and openness in order for the story to have maximum impact.

NURTURING THE IMAGINATION

Common people and theorists alike have used story to inform learning in families, schools, and communities. We present the following story within that construct, and want to privilege and highlight this process by taking the reader into our lives as we share our work visually, in narrative, and in practice. Using storytelling as a process for community change requires imagining the future while we also share the past and frame the present. The oral story, unlike traditional writing, is rarely linear, or predictable, or bound by the APA manual on style. The process of story at times takes on the identity and feel of a roller coaster, with its usual peaks and valleys. At times, like the most dramatic of steep drops, it is embellished with local flavor, with the unimaginable, with the absurd. We, like other storytellers, have been accused of falling prey to the occasional hyperbole. Traditional academic settings do not always privilege the storytelling process, but there is no doubt that the ability to understand, to construct and to tell a good story creates power in people, in their work, and in community. Our experience tells us that the use of story is perhaps the most effective teaching and learning strategy in our communities. It has enabled us to imagine the world within a different context and with different possibilities.

THE LLANO GRANDE STORY: CULTIVATING A COMMUNITY NARRATIVE

The story of the Llano Grande Center is a story of long-term incubation of visions and dreams. It is a story that holds ideas and lessons learned by listening to the stories of our parents, as well as by self-organizing our own baseball leagues during summers while growing up in rural south Texas. It is a story shaped by the imagining of a better story for ourselves and our community. As kids, we weren't calling anything Llano Grande, we simply played the roles of normal, energetic children who obeyed our parents, and who grew up in a town where people cared for us. Those are ideas and memories that fueled the passion for what would years later become the Llano Grande Center for Research and Development.

When we left home to go to college in the early 1980s, we took friends from our hometowns of Elsa and Edcouch with us, and found other friends from other parts of the world. While in college, the story that one day we would come back home to take part in rebuilding our community began to take shape. The dream became clearer after college, when we returned. We came back with a renewed sense of self, and were more global in our thinking; we had grown up a bit more at the university in the big city, had studied abroad, and traveled to several continents of the world. By the early 1990s, our love for our hometown, devotion to the stories of our childhood, and lessons learned from our formal studies and travels, melded into a clearer vision. The vision gained greater clarity when we began to enact some of our life-long ideas in the classrooms at Edcouch-Elsa High School. These were ideas about building our own stories as individuals and as members of a community, and about doing that with students through the use of specific curricular and pedagogical approaches such as the collecting of oral histories, using the tools of ethnographic study, and engaging in other community-based research practices.

Coming back home was somewhat complicated. It was such a gift and opportunity, but it was also a challenge. Our upbringing had taught us the power of the stories, the wisdom and compassion of the people, and the charm in the narrative of the town itself. All that defined the opportunity. The challenge was that most townspeople did not see their story as an asset, as a source of personal power, nor did they view their community as a unique and special place. Students at the high school mirrored this perspective; they were mired in a notion that they could not dream big about going to a good college. The sense of low expectations was palpable, even seemed endemic. Much of this stemmed from the socio-economic condition of the community and region.

For more than a generation, this region held the dubious distinction of being the most economically impoverished area in the country. The steady influx of immigrants from south of the Texas-Mexico border populated the region with people of limited economic or other material means. The place and region gained a clear identity as a result of a century-long agricultural economy that essentially defined a two-tiered economic and social structure comprised of (1) a ruling class and (2) a working class. We were raised in this two-tiered society and were full participants in it, along with our parents and extended family. We were the workers in the agricultural fields; this is the reality that shaped us.

This setting also cultivated a dominant narrative in our community. It was a narrative of power, a macro-story where the landowners and farmers wielded power, and manual workers followed their orders. This socio-economic dynamic was largely informed by race, as Anglos (whites) made up the vast majority of the ruling class, while Mexicans and Mexican Americans populated the working class. Social structures and life similarly reflected the two-tiered system in ways that starkly resembled "Jim Crow" laws of the American South. Segregation reigned supreme: there was a school for white children, and a separate "Mexican" school; the white theater, and the *Cine Mexicano*. This was the South, after all, as much as it was the American Southwest. The economic and social conditions supported the dominant narrative, and in that narrative Mexican and Mexican American children were not supposed to think about going to college, much less an exclusive college—that notion was directly opposed to the unspoken but widely accepted storyline.

Slowly, however, that narrative began to crack. Mexican American students began to attend college. Typically, though, they only thought about the possibility of going to technical school, or to the local college. In this emerging story of college, there was little space for Mexican American students to leap far beyond the base expectation. The psychological impact of the two-tiered society engrained in the minds of many local people the idea that they could not reach high, could not dream big. This was a social construction that had to be reversed. In contrast, our thinking was governed by the stories we heard as children, stories generated through the same social and economic structures, but told and understood in radically different ways; stories quite different from those told by those in power. This was the antithesis to the dominant narrative—it was the part that we were exposed to as kids, and it was a gorgeous gift.

The counter-story was the part that our parents and elders shared with us. They told about how they worked tirelessly to clear the tough south Texas brush to build new towns; they told stories of how they worked the agricultural fields in order to feed their families; they also told of how they fed an entire nation. We heard stories of hard-working people who persevered in the face of adversity, raised healthy and well-adjusted families, and participated in most facets of social and civic life. The range of stories was impressive, as were the multiple genres used to tell the stories: jokes, songs, poems, platicas (conversations), and as our father called them, "trajedias y comedias." The stories were told around the dinner table, on the front porch, sometimes at the local coffee shop. On occasion, we learned from stories transmitted through the radio, though

Llano Grande collective leadership fellows. Photo by Eddie Rios

those were often filtered through our parents. These were genuine stories of the human spirit. They were real "American" stories.

This part of the narrative was not typically talked about in schools, or in the popular media, nor were they reflected in the market culture. But this was the uplifting part of the broader narrative, the part that could inspire children, and elders, and move communities that had been mired in social and economic degradation, toward a new, a more enlightened existence. Our challenge was to rehabilitate the dominant narrative, and we saw the school as an appropriate laboratory through which to experiment with making those changes. We felt a responsibility to employ the lessons we had learned from our elders, from the rest of our community, and through our higher education experience. We would use the combination of these lessons to build a formal pedagogy that would instruct, but also emerge as a community development strategy.

We felt we had to take a big leap if we were to change the community story in a bold way. Our challenge was to use the stories to cultivate a new kind of expectation for students, and, by extension, to raise the collective level of expectation of the community. From a college preparation standpoint, we decided to prepare our students so they could get into universities such as Harvard, Yale, Columbia, Stanford, and MIT. And so we went to work, building a curriculum to do just that: a curriculum that was grounded in the exploration of story, in identity formation, in community-based research of the community's history and resources, in part through the collection of the community's stories—all that becoming the curricular framework through which students learned the 3Rs. We believed our students from this community, many who came from immigrant and/or migrant families, possessed the talent and ability to do well in the best colleges in the country. Beyond building the academic skills, they just had to believe they could.

To a large extent, community elders helped our students, our teachers, and the school to see things differently. They held the key to the treasure chest of stories, but we just didn't know it—not until we started to engage them in storytelling. Our youth had begun to collect oral histories from elders in the community, and one day we visited an elder named Jose Isabel Gutierrez, who was particularly critical in laying down a framework for a counter-story. When a high school class went to interview this ninety-seven-year-old elder at his home, it didn't take him but fifteen minutes into the storytelling session before he asserted himself as a founder of the town of Edcouch.

The students were baffled by the elder's proclamation. He had clearly worked as a laborer his entire life, as evidenced not just by his callused hands and worn body, but also by stories he shared in the first few minutes. When he announced himself as a "founder of Edcouch," one student asked him why he called himself that. Mr. Gutierrez responded by asking the youngster, "Have you ever had any water in Edcouch?" The youngster said, "Yes, I have." To which, the elder responded, "In 1927, I dug the ditches to lay down the water pipes for the town of Edcouch ... *Yo soy fundador de Edcouch* (I am a founder of Edcouch)." With that story, Mr. Gutierrez turned the community narrative on its head. As this working class man assigned himself agency as a notable historical character, he also gave himself, and everyone who shared his experience, political power as founder and builder of the community. This kind of assertion had been missing from the narrative of the town, and we began to find it as we sought out the stories of the elders.

The stories catalyzed the college preparation work, particularly as students began to see how the power in the stories of the elders could also become power in their own stories. Generating power from student stories then emerged as a cornerstone of the college preparation process. That is when the broader community narrative began to shift. And almost two decades later, after placing dozens of students in Ivy League universities, and after raising the college-going rate of graduating seniors from Edcouch-Elsa High School by more than 100 percent, a new narrative has gained traction. Today, local youth feel as if they have the permission to dream big about where to go to college, and about what they want to do with their lives. As importantly, many students now view their community as a place with value, and many imagine better days to come. The two-tiered story has given way to a more egalitarian social and economic construct where more local residents, including youth, participate in the life of their community. The story of the two-tiered structure was driven by a few who made decisions about economy, education, and local policy. The new narrative is an emerging model where collective leadership and action are seen as important means to community change.

The story of the Llano Grande is a story of building power, built on the strengths and wisdom of local people, both young and old, and a story that boldly places those who have been historically marginalized at the center of constructing new meaning.

BIRTHING THE STORY OF CHANGE

The story of the Llano Grande Center and its work with other groups committed to collective leadership has evolved during the past few years into a body of work called the Community Learning Exchange (CLE), which you have heard about in other places in this book. During a recent CLE, hosted by organizations in Minnesota and Northwest Wisconsin, and held along the St. Croix River, the group of participants gathered in a

Olga Cardozo-Vasquez and her husband, Omar Vasquez, a few months after their baby, Izcali, was born. Photo by Cheryl D. Fields

circle to offer closing reflections. One participant, a young woman named Olga who happened to be seven months pregnant, shared her testimony with others. As she prepared to speak, she rubbed the underside of her belly, gently caressing her unborn child. She then said, "I'm very emotional right now. It may be because I'm about to give birth, but I think it's also because I feel so grateful to everyone here because you represent a caring and nurturing society that I will be bringing my baby into in just a few months. ... I just want to thank you for reminding me of that." As she said that, Olga and the rest of us looked at each other, collectively closing the chapter on yet another story of community change.

CONCLUSION

If you want to go fast, go alone.
If you want to go far, go with others.
— AFRICAN PROVERB

Photo by Cheryl D. Fields

One of the challenges of this book has been trying to decide what to include. There have been so many stories and lessons emerging from our work over the last decade. And so many changes have happened within our communities as a result of practicing collective leadership. It took us a while to find the essential heart of what we hope will be of service to others.

We kept coming back to the realization that what maintains the connection among this community of activists is the depth of relationships, the beauty of learning from those with different experiences, the trust we have in the wisdom of our communities and the stories that make

105

us laugh, connect, dream and feel inspired. We have learned that what makes this work matter is that it is a way of life that transforms everyone who becomes involved. Elayne Dorsey, one of the national team members, describes what happened to her as she embraced this way of life. "It is amazing to me how much the collective leadership model is just a part of who I am now—sometimes I just forget that there is another way and that people still believe that the big boss and his/her little team are the ones with all the answers and should be the only ones with all the information. When people believe that old way, it is very difficult for them to share or to let go of the perceived power of being the ones with all the answers."

Sometimes it is hard to look at how our current systems and institutions are failing to serve so many of us and not feel discouraged and hopeless about the inequities and the challenges we face. Those of us interested in community change work yearn for a new social fabric. We yearn for a social cohesion based in belonging, inclusion, interdependence, security, recognition, and legitimacy for all of us.

Those of us interested in collective leadership know it is possible because we are experiencing it. We can see it when we come together. Each person picks up a thread of what is unraveling in our social fabric and re-weaves it into the whole cloth we want for all of us. As we do, we create a new social fabric that reflects the values and ways of working together described in this book. And in the process, we inspire each other.

Collective leadership is not for the faint of heart. It is hard work to stand in difficult places and look for solutions, to face our fears and find our partners, and to bring about changes that make life better for all members of our community. Yet, collective leadership increases our individual and collective capacity to do this hard work.

Capacity building is a natural outcome of collective leadership. It occurs as the individuals involved increase their confidence and develop their skills. It occurs as the group members increases their effectiveness in working together and making best use of available resources, including all the newly uncovered talents of individuals. This is a mutually reinforcing cycle—stronger individuals make for a stronger group, and a stronger group supports the growth of individuals. And, because these patterns are life-giving, more and more people become connected. This is another form of increased capacity.

Ginger Alferos, part of the Mi Casa leadership team, described how her life changed when this work moved from being her job to the way she wanted to be in the world. It was at that point that she took full owner-ship for her own learning and behavior. As she lived the principles of collective leadership and built them into all the programs she managed, she blossomed, as did the people around her and the results of their work together.

Living the principles of collective leadership requires a willingness to stay in a place of learning and inquiry. We cannot successfully engage each other in the ways we talk about in this book unless we are willing to let go of old assumptions and beliefs, and unless we can maintain open minds and listening hearts. We practitioners of this kind of leadership start our work not with an answer but with a question.

In this state of openness, we find ourselves able to adapt to emerging opportunities. Traditionally, a small leadership group relies on detailed plans to address its long-term goals. In contrast, we have come to expect that surprising and better approaches to arrive at a goal will often unfold as we attend to what each of us brings to the table, both in terms of gifts and insights. Collective leadership empowers individuals to take action when they see something that will advance the work of the group—communicating and checking in as needed. Taking ownership and initiative is encouraged by all. As Elayne implied in her quote, co-workers are partners in the work, whatever their position. The stories in this book are filled with instances where a group, open to the moment, experienced a change of heart or a change of plans.

One ongoing benefit to being a collective leader is that no one person is expected to have all the answers, to take on all the responsibility, or to figure out alone why things didn't work the expected way. One of the great joys of this work is the camaraderie of joining with others who share your passion and your desire to make your place better. One of the great joys is being in relationships that truly share sorrow and setbacks as well as celebration and success.

A recurrent theme that runs through these stories is how inspirational and helpful it is to take a break from the intense and sometimes isolating daily efforts of this work to gather with others from distant communities. The storytellers make frequent reference to national gatherings and community learning exchanges. These gatherings have offered an opportunity to share stories and to learn from others what they are doing, to give and receive support and friendship. The beginning of the Resources section tells about the Community Learning Exchange (CLE) so often referred to in this book. The CLE is a place where you can find your peer learning community. We hope that you will join us—either online in our virtual setting or on-the-ground in face-to-face exchanges.

In this book on collective leadership, we have named four patterns of working together that, when adopted by a community, transform it. Kwesi Rollins, another national team member, offers a closing thought on how important this work is to our country.

"As our stories indicate, collective leadership and community change are personally enriching and life changing. But this is also challenging work, particularly in our world today. As we finish this wonderful storybook, we are aware of how frequently communities have become polarized around difficult issues like immigration. Additionally, the turmoil across the country over plans to build an Islamic cultural center near ground zero, the former site of the World Trade Center in New York City, stirred up ugly anti-Muslim sentiments not only across New York City but in other parts of the country, leading to acts of vandalism and violence. A lack of understanding of and respect for different religious and cultural practices coupled with a lack of peaceful, constructive dialogue breeds intolerance. This polarization is a stark reminder of what can happen when old hurts remain unhealed (in this case the 9-11 attacks on the World Trade Center) and are allowed to fester, sowing further division. Our stories reveal the power and potential of turning moments of division into times of healing and learning together."

DELIVERING A MANIFESTO:
A CONVERSATION BETWEEN AN ELDER AND A YOUTH

by Francisco Guajardo

(an imaginary exchange based on true events)

"Building Community" by Delvis Cortes.

A young man named Martin walks next to an elder named Jorge. Martin refers to the elder as "Don" Jorge, "Don" used as a title showing respect in many Latin American cultures. At the time of this encounter, Martin is in his 20s and Jorge is in his 60s. They became acquainted and formed a strong bond a few years earlier when they had worked together as part of a community group that wanted to make changes in their rural hometown. The group they belonged to was committed to including voices of all ages in their efforts—both the making of decisions and the taking of actions were carried out in a truly cross-generational way.

Though they haven't seen each other in quite some time, the genuine pleasure in their greeting reflects a deep connection.

Martin: Buenos dias, Don Jorge. It's been a while since I last saw you. How are you? I've missed you.

Jorge: I'm doing well, Martin. I have missed your company, too. I have very good memories about the work we did together a few years ago. We need to do more of that. In fact, I'm just now working on doing the same with others from the community. I'm on my way to the Molcajete Café to read a letter to a group who will be gathering there this afternoon.

Martin: A letter? I'm intrigued, Don Jorge. Will you tell me more?

Jorge: Yes, Martin. Walk with me, and I'll tell you about it. I think you'll like what's in the letter, because it's actually about the work you and I were involved in a few years ago, when you were still a teenager. It's the story of our work building community leadership. I suppose we could even say that this letter is a manifesto, a call to our community people to work together, using the lessons we learned about collective leadership.

Martin: Please continue, Don Jorge. I love talking about all we learned together, and about the way we joined with so many others to build our community leadership capacity. It was such a special experience to watch people who were never involved in their community learn that they had so much to offer. So tell me, how did you construct your story? What stories do you write about to tell the bigger story?

Jorge: Well, Martin, as you know, I am an old man, and I have lived through many stories. So first, I tell certain stories that took place in this community decades ago. Those stories are important because they've given us an identity; they've given us a sense of place.

Martin: Yes, I like that. You and other elders have taught us that the stories of the past are very important. Those smaller stories are the building blocks of the broader narrative of our community today.

Jorge: But I also include newer stories.

Martin's phone buzzes, as the young man and the elder continue their walk.

Martin: Excuse me, Don Jorge. I'm getting a text message from my mother. It'll take me just a few seconds to tell her I'll be home a bit later than expected.

Jorge: I tell a story about that, Martin.

Martin: About what? Texting?

Jorge: Yes, about how you and your peers use technology so much. You're using your cell phone to text right now; you use your computer to get on the Internet, probably every day. Some of us older people have learned so much about how young people communicate and network these days. I recall when you and other teenagers just a few years ago used social networking websites to encourage teenagers to get out to vote. You remember how we won funding to build new schools, in part because so many eighteen- and nineteen-year-olds voted yes to the bond issue. That's an important lesson on how to expand collective action through the use of technology. We have learned that from you and other young people.

Martin: I remember how good that felt, encouraging community youth to exercise their right to vote, inviting young people to a life of civic participation. And I think the way so many were involved is such a great example of effective community leadership. We changed our community through that experience.

Jorge: That lesson is not lost in my letter, Martin.

Martin: I'm happy to hear that, Don Jorge. Please tell me more about the letter.

Jorge: I'd be happy to. You remember, Martin, that one of the first lessons we learned about effective and sustainable leadership is that before we engage in any initiatives to change the community, we must first spend time getting to know each other. We must first invest in building relation-ships, and in building trust. I remember the conversations with you about how that process was an essential part of changing any community.

Martin: I remember that clearly, Don Jorge. I was so frustrated. I wanted to jump straight into the work. It took a while to realize that building relationships and trust is actually the most critical work we can do to transform ourselves and our community. That was a key lesson we all learned together.

Jorge: That lesson is in my letter. I emphasize it in a big and bold way.

Martin: I am glad to hear that. How about the lesson of moving away from the historic reliance on the individual leader ... you know, the Lone Ranger model of leadership? Do you include something in the letter about that?

Jorge: I do indeed. It's another point of emphasis, and I make the point by telling the story of the school principal who realized that leading through charisma and individual talent was not sufficient. As that principal went through our leadership experience, he quickly understood that his being an effective leader was intimately tied to how involved his faculty and staff were in the planning and the work. When he helped them develop their leadership capacity, he found that everyone, including himself, could better understand and address their shared issues. He learned the lesson that leading with others was far more useful than leading by himself.

Martin: Yes. He discovered that the best way he could put his personal gifts to use was to build the collective leadership at his school. But it wasn't just the school principal. There were many who realized that leading with others is a much better leadership style and method than leading by oneself.

Jorge: That, my young friend, is the essence of collective leadership. It is also at the center of building a strong democratic society—another main point in my letter.

Martin: I suspect mention of a good democracy is in your letter as well?

Jorge: It is.

Martin: What else is in the letter?

Jorge: Probably the hardest to change, as you know, Martin, are the systems that we work in. You remember our conversations with other community people about how to change the school, or how to change policy, or how to re-shape the institutions that have so much power over common people. My letter says a great deal about that, but it also looks at the issue in a very sobering way. Changing the system has been the toughest thing, but I think you and I will agree the best way to do that is through collective action. Would you say that's true?

Martin: Yes, that is my experience, too.

The two friends come to an abrupt stop, a pause from their walk, and share in a moment of deep reflection. Then Martin breaks the silence.

Martin: There is something else I hope is in your letter. Something about how doing this work changes us.

Jorge: That is maybe the biggest point made in the letter—that all these parts to collective leadership that I have talked about—building relationships, building trust, valuing story, drawing on everyone's wisdom—they must become a part of our way of life, and when that happens, something authentic and powerful happens. I include that in the letter.

Martin: Wow, Don Jorge, it sounds like you have crafted a powerful letter. I'd love to be at that meeting.

Jorge: Well, why don't you come with me to the Molcajete Café? More than that, I'd like to deliver the contents of this letter in partnership with you, Martin. Since your stories are part of my story, I think it would be good testimony to teamwork, to collaboration, and to collective leadership.

Martin: I would be proud to do that. First, I'll need to tell my mother where I'll be. Gracias, Don Jorge, for that very kind invitation. We're sure to have some fun.

Martin texts his mother as he and Don Jorge walk to the Molcajete Café. When they arrive at the coffee shop, it is filled with locals. There Martin and Jorge deliver their manifesto on collective leadership for community change. As they do, they engage everyone in a conversation on community, leadership, and other issues important to those in attendance. It is a good evening for the community.

RESOURCES

THE COMMUNITY LEARNING EXCHANGE

The Community Learning Exchange (CLE) is a network of resilient local communities, vibrant organizations, and active change agents who share their local wisdom and collective leadership approaches with each other so that they can be more effective in addressing critical social issues.

We envision a world in which community challenges are addressed, not by individual leaders, but by collective leadership—groups of local residents working together for sustainable change in 21st century settings. Unlike conventional learning institutions, which may be grounded in formal teaching practices and offer a curriculum delivered by credentialed experts and supported by academic texts, the Community Learning Exchange views communities and people as the new instructors and texts for learning. It encourages community change agents to share actions, practices, ideas, and outcomes with one another in environments that respect and value local wisdom.

The CLE is a growing network that connects local communities, organizations and change agents across the U.S. through three-day learning exchanges, an online networking website and thought-leader gatherings. It provides an opportunity for community leadership groups to openly examine their challenges, to freely exchange successful approaches and to become familiar with tools that can enhance local change initiatives. Community organizations host learning exchanges that illuminate how local history and context affect local challenges and the approaches used to address such social change topics as educational equity, immigrant rights, health, poverty, and structural racism. Participants are encouraged to attend in teams to make follow-up implementation of action plans more practical.

Teams come from communities grappling with similar issues, cohort groups supported by various funder initiatives, and networks connected to specific social change issues. The topics for each learning exchange emerge from the interests of communities in the network and from other groups wanting to become part of the network. We welcome participation from new funder initiatives, communities who want to break their isolation and groups/networks working on specific change initiatives.

Information about the Community Learning Exchange is available at: http://www.communitylearningexchange.org or by contacting the Center for Ethical Leadership at 206-328-3020.

SUPPORT MATERIALS FOR IMPLEMENTING COLLECTIVE LEADERSHIP

The Collective Leadership Framework: A Workbook For Cultivating And Sustaining Community Change

The Framework is a tool for groups interested in achieving sustainable community change through the process of collective leadership. The Framework is a matrix created by the Center for Ethical Leadership and the Institute for Educational Leadership that guides you through this work. The workbook provides an overall explanation of the Framework along with worksheets to take you step-by-step through the process.

It is available through the Center for Ethical Leadership, www.ethicalleadership.org, or by calling 206-328-3020.

Collective Leadership Works: Preparing Youth and Adults for Community Change

This toolkit shares and expands on activities and approaches used during the KLCC session on valuing and building youth and adult partnerships. It was developed by the Innovation Center for Community and Youth Development.

It is available through the Innovation Center's website, www.theinnovationcenter.org, or by calling 301-270-1700.

GRACIOUS SPACE: THE PRIMER
by Karma Ruder

Chapter 1 shared many stories about Gracious Space in action. This primer shares the basics of the methodology. We can explain Gracious Space in five minutes, although it can take a lifetime of practice to perfect. This is the five minute explanation!

Gracious Space enables us to form deeper relationships that are open and respectful so that we can have the tough conversations needed to move through stuck places and to open up new possibilities. Gracious Space offers its practitioners transformative change. What it asks of us is that we candidly and honestly develop ourselves so that we can bring our best selves to how we relate to others who share a common purpose.

Within any geographic location, there are many communities, not just one. These communities can be organized around a physical neighborhood, a shared cultural or ethnic experience, or a specific common interest. Each of these communities has a different story about what has happened in the past and why. When people with very different stories come together, they often bump into each other and experience conflict or stress. This is true even when they agree on the shared goal of changing an institution or system that does not sufficiently serve any of them. Gracious Space enables people to stay in those tensions that are a part of every effort to make a change. This, in turn, encourages the group to find vibrant new solutions, rather than falling back into old compromises.

THE ELEMENTS

We have all had experiences of Gracious Space, though we may have called it by other names. The Center for Ethical Leadership defines Gracious Space as: "A spirit and setting in which we invite the stranger and learn in public."

That definition calls out each of the four elements of Gracious Space—spirit, setting, inviting the stranger, and learning in public. These elements are simple to understand, although not necessarily easy to put into practice. Living into Gracious Space requires a level of attention and intention that comes from either great heart or great mindfulness. Below is a simple introduction to the four elements.

Spirit

Gracious Space has many aspects, such as welcoming, compassion, curiosity and humor. Each of us carries many of these qualities. When we bring them with us into our relationships, we are "being" Gracious Space. This spirit is what sets Gracious Space apart from other communication or conflict resolution tools. Gracious Space is about preparing ourselves to bring our best intention into every interaction, and drawing out the best intentions and spirit of others.

Setting

Gracious Space also has a physical dimension. The space we use for meetings needs to support our ability to feel productive, healthy, safe, and connected to our work and to each other. Paying attention to simple hospitality (food, drink, room temperature) and providing items that reflect the energy and personality of the group (art, music, natural beauty) contribute to a gracious environment. This element also has an aspect of time to it. For example, when we set up a meeting, we match the length of the agenda to the time available so that we can productively engage each other.

Invite the stranger

The term "stranger" refers to any individual who is not typically involved in the conversation: someone with a different background, perspective, skin color, gender, geographic orientation, or any other quality that may make them seem different. The stranger can also be any idea or perspective that is different than the one we hold. We need the stranger when we are considering complex and new ideas. Our decision-making processes benefit from multiple perspectives that broaden our viewpoints. Otherwise, we may take actions that are too narrow-minded, or have only short-term benefits. Inviting the stranger is a strategic decision that opens up more possibilities. We also need the stranger if we are to create communities that benefit all members. And it's good to remember that we are each the stranger to someone else, and perhaps even to parts of ourselves.

Learn in public

Gracious Space asks us to engage in deep listening—with a commitment to learn—as part of the diverse group we have gathered into Gracious Space. Learning in public requires humility, a willingness to explore assumptions and let go of the "right way" of doing things, and a willingness to change our minds and open our hearts. It also means being willing to express—in a respectful way—our own thoughts and feelings that others need to hear to understand and learn from us.

These four elements of Gracious Space create conditions for people to be fully alive, fully engaged, and fully present. In his book Theory U, innovation theorist Otto Scharmer tells us, "Successful leadership depends on the quality of attention and intention that the leader brings to any situation. Two leaders in the same circumstances doing the same thing can bring about completely different outcomes, depending on the inner place from which each operates."[6]

---

6 Scharmer, Otto. (2007). "Addressing the Blind Spot of Our Time": an executive summary of Scharmer's book: *Theory U: Leading from the Future as It Emerges.* Cambridge: Society for Organizational Learning, pg. 1 www.theoryU.com.

The creativity that emerges when people come together from a place of joy and connectedness is more likely to lead to good solutions.

GETTING STARTED

Filled with a sense of urgency, many groups jump into action without taking the time to learn each other's stories, to understand the wounds of the past with empathy, or to identify what kinds of processes bring out the best in each other. Sometimes, groups do not take the time to consider the different meanings of words routinely used, assuming that everyone understands them the same way. We have learned that rushing past this foundation-building work is a costly mistake.

Here are some simple ways to engage Gracious Space in meetings:

Start in a good way

Take time for everyone to become present in his/her spirit, and the spirit of Gracious Space, and to remain open to learning in public.

Examples of quick methods include:

- Take three deep breaths together before starting. Neurologically, this causes the brain to let go of stress and to become calmer.
- Check in with a question such as, "What energy are you bringing into this meeting?" or, "What is your intention for what you want to bring to this conversation?"

If a difficult conversation is coming up, it is worth spending time to create an environment that encourages sharing thoughts in a good way:

- As the first step, invite people to name what is most important to them about the issue.
- Begin with a written reflection to allow participants to prepare themselves to share their key hopes and concerns.

Ask questions that open up possibilities before getting to solutions

Compelling questions can shift a conversation from one that drains spirit to one that opens people up and generates new ideas. While it is always good to ask questions that are specific to your meeting, here are a few general questions that work with inviting the stranger and learning in public:

- What boundaries need to be crossed for the work to move to the next level?
- What are we doing that is undermining what we want to accomplish?
- What do we need to let go of to make room for something new?
- What is so important that it must exist in some way for this effort to succeed?

Make room for storytelling

When dealing only with ideas and opinions, it is very easy to move into judgment. However, telling stories that share experience leaves less room for judgment because the truth is in the story itself. Making time for participants to share how they have become the people they are, why they care about a particular issue, or what their experience has been with a particular issue, will open up understanding and spark deeper connection. This is an easy way to invite the stranger.

Take time for sharing reflection

A meeting that consists only of moving through agenda items and tasks can reflect a sense of urgency and foster a belief that there isn't enough time. Creating time for reflection—even a few minutes—invites people to move from the dance floor to the balcony.[7] It is from the balcony that we can reflect on what is working or what isn't, and on our role and behavior. In this way, we can more clearly see what the group might do to improve results. Time for reflection increases the ability to learn in public.

In one group, when the situation heated up and people started talking over one another, someone would call out, "Gracious Space" as a reminder for everyone to slow down, listen to each other, and take a step back to look at what was going on in the group.

Close in a good way

In closing a meeting, have a checkout round so that no one has to imagine what others are feeling. The checkout round helps the meeting end with a good spirit as people exit or, alternatively, generates a good set of questions for the next meeting. Examples of checkout questions are:

- What one word, phrase, or sentence describes your experience of this meeting?
- What are you taking away as a result of this conversation?

RESOURCES

Hughes, Patricia M. (2004). *Gracious Space: A Practical Guide for Working Together Better.* Center for Ethical Leadership.

Hughes, Patricia M.; Ruder, Karma; Nienow, Dale. (Expected 2011). *Using Gracious Space to Support Transformative Change Processes (Working title).*

7 Heifetz, Ronald. (1998). *Leadership Without Easy Answers.* Massachusetts: Harvard University Press, pg. 253

The Gracious Space Practitioner Group can be joined through the Community Learning Exchange at www.communitylearningexchange.org.

For a schedule of upcoming Gracious Space trainings visit the Center for Ethical Leadership's website at www.ethicalleadership.org.

CIRCLES: AN INTRODUCTION
from "The Manual for Circle Keepers" by Roca Inc.

UNDERSTANDING AND DESCRIBING CIRCLES

The circle is a process that brings together individuals who wish to engage in conflict resolution, healing, support, decision making, or other activities in which honest communication, relationship development, and community building are core desired outcomes.

"Circles" offer an alternative to contemporary meeting processes that often rely on hierarchy, win-lose positioning, and victim/rescuer approaches to relationships and problem solving.

Derived from aboriginal and native traditions, circles bring people together in a way that creates trust, intimacy, goodwill, belonging, generosity, mutuality, and reciprocity. The process is never about "changing others," but rather is a gentle invitation to change one's relationship with oneself, to the community and to the wider universe.

Circles intentionally create a sacred space that lifts barriers between people, opening fresh possibilities for connection, collaboration, and mutual understanding. The process works because it brings people together in a way that allows them to see one another as human beings and to talk about what matters.

Circles can be understood in terms of the values and principles upon which they operate, and the structures they use to support these values and principles.

Values and principles

Though each circle develops its own values and principles, all peacemaking circles generally:

- are designed by those who use them
- are guided by a shared vision
- call participants to act on their personal values
- include all interests, and are accessible to all

- offer everyone an equal, and voluntary, opportunity to participate
- take a holistic approach, including the emotional, mental, physical, and spiritual
- maintain respect for all
- encourage exploring instead of conquering differences
- invite accountability to others and to the process

Structure

Circles provide gentle, highly effective support to groups seeking to stay on course with the values and principles they have established for their circle. The circle process is "simple but not easy." There are some key structures that help to define the circle.

- In the meeting space participants are seated in a circle. The center of the circle may contain symbolic objects that help remind participants of shared values, or may relate to the purpose of the particular circle. The center of the circle may also be kept empty.
- A talking piece is used as a way to ensure respect between speakers and listeners. The talking piece is passed from person to person within the circle and only the person holding the piece may speak.
- A keeper of the circle guides the participants and creates and holds the circle as a unique and safe space. Keepers are qualified to lead circle if they have experienced circles themselves and/or if they have been trained in the process.
- Ceremony and ritual are used to create safety and form.
- Consensus decision making honors the values and principles of peacemaking circles, and helps participants to stay grounded in them. All needs are heard and the group commits to addressing them in some manner.

Circles can be used to provide emotional or spiritual support to individuals, to create an open dialogue around specific topics, or as a way of making decisions in many settings.

Grounding the circle in the medicine wheel

Aboriginal and native people in particular have kept the medicine wheel at the heart of their lives. The practice of circles is grounded in the tradition of the medicine wheel. The medicine wheel is built upon the natural phenomenon of things occurring in "fours" (i.e., seasons, phases of the moon, stages of life) to suggest that there are four components of individual and community health: physical, mental, emotional, and spiritual.

If things are going wrong in the life of an individual or of a community, the circle offers a way to examine where there may be an imbalance in the physical, mental, emotional or spiritual dimension of the individual or community. In seeking to bring an individual or community back

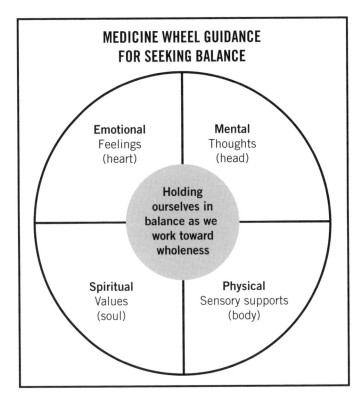

into balance, circles use a four-stage process that brings people together to get to know one another on deep levels. People learn to trust one another so that they may move through issues and toward solutions. An inevitable outcome of the process is healing, relationship building, and community building.

Seven key principles of circle are:
1. Circles are not a thing or a program, but a way to be.
2. Circles are a sacred space.
3. Circles are about giving oneself up and sharing to help others.
4. Circles foster accountability.

5. No one controls circle; they are spaces of collective empowerment.
6. Circles are about the invitation; no one can be forced to sit in circle.
7. Circle is not about circle; it is about us.

While circles have been adapted for many communities and to serve many purposes, they share essential features:
- Everyone in the circle is equal and has equal opportunity to speak.
- Decisions are made by consensus.
- Everyone agrees to abide by guidelines established by the group based on shared values in order to work toward a common goal.

A GUIDE TO SERVING AS A CIRCLE KEEPER
Before keeping circle ask yourself:
- Am I striving to exhibit keeper traits?
- Am I doing my inner work?
- Do I know my 'stuff'?
- Am I the best person to keep this circle?
- Am I taking care of myself in a balanced way?
- Do I understand the circle process?
- Do I trust the process?

What is a circle keeper?
Keepers are also known as servants, facilitators, carriers, and other names. Whatever name is used, the role is the same. Keepers are the caretakers and servants of the process. As a keeper, you must ensure that everyone takes responsibility for helping to keep the circle, and for making the circle a safe place for open dialogue.

Qualities of the keeper—Am I striving to exhibit keeper traits?
When you agree to serve as a circle keeper, you are taking on a sacred trust. It can feel intimidating at first. So the first thing to remember is to relax, and to forgive yourself for being imperfectly human as we all are. No keeper is perfect. We do the best we can.

Here are some traits that can help you to best serve the circle. Remember, none of us are perfect at all of these things. But if you keep them in mind as you move into your keeper role, they will serve you and the circle.

- A good listener
- Present
- Supportive
- Nonjudgmental
- Fair
- Inclusive

- Courageous
- Organized
- Able to keep the process moving
- Detached
- Appreciative
- Patient
- Well-disciplined
- Watchful
- Approachable
- Reflective
- Trusting
- Encouraging
- Respectful
- Aware
- Tolerant
- Humble
- Holistic
- Able to appreciate humor
- Open to other opinions
- Honest
- An anchor
- Willing to forgive
- Consistently flexible
- Able to keep the space safe

The keeper is responsible for holding three stages: before, during and after the circle.

BEFORE THE CIRCLE

Determine suitability
When deciding whether or not to use circles consider:
- what the goals for a circle would be
- if a circle is really suitable, appropriate for the situation at hand
- if there are people who would be willing and able to sit in circle
- if there are people who can and/or could keep a circle
- if there are resources to support a circle (space, food, supplies, etc.)

Prepare others for the circle
Before the gathering, keepers work together to prepare others for the circle. Remember that participation in circle is an invitation. Keepers:
- help identify who needs to be there
- explain to participants how circles work and the role as keeper
- find out what are the issues, concerns, and needs
- discuss guidelines and ask participants what guidelines will make the circle safe for them
- begin building relationships with participants

Handle logistics
Keepers determine:
- *Time*—Choose a time that will be convenient for the most participants.

- *Place*—Choose a place that is neutral and that will support all participants in feeling equal and safe.
- *Participants*—Remember you cannot force anyone to come to circle.
- *Talking piece*—Choose something that will have meaning for the participants.
- *Materials*—Have markers, easels, a talking piece, and materials for the center.
- *Refreshments*—Have refreshments available for circle.
- *Cultural sensitivity*—Be sensitive to the special needs and requirements of different cultures.

DURING THE CIRCLE

As keeper, you are responsible for creating and keeping the "form" of the circle. You act as a guide as you move the circle through the phases it needs to experience. These five phases are flexible depending on the purpose for which a circle has been called. However, it is important that all circles include phase one (grounding) and phase five (closing), and that these two phases are always given time and depth.

Five phases of circles

Although the content or topical focus of circles may vary, all circles generally follow five phases. How you facilitate these phases is flexible. For example, a new group may need to spend more time on guidelines and on the storytelling round. Trust your instincts on how to structure phase one.

The five phases of the circle process are:

1. Grounding
2. Deepening
3. Exploring options
4. Building consensus or a sense of unity
5. Closing

Phase One—Grounding. The grounding phase of circle may include the following elements, all of which are designed to create safety and form, and to begin to prepare participants for deeper sharing and understanding. This phase generally should include the following:

- Welcoming—Make sure everyone is greeted warmly.

- Opening ceremony—All circles start with an opening ceremony that helps us to make the transition from the outer world into the reflective circle space. Openings should help us feel more centered and open to inner peace and deep sharing. Openings may involve burning sage or incense, which someone either places in the middle of the circle or passes over participants, using a feather to move the smoke around them, allowing people to cleanse themselves of negative energies and to prepare for sharing deeper emotions. The openings may include a poem, song, or meditative music. Consider asking one of the participants, in advance, to offer the opening.

- Introductions and check-in—In the first round, keepers ask participants to introduce themselves by name, how they feel, why they are present and what they hope to achieve.

- Seeking consensus around guidelines—If it is a new group, participants develop guidelines for how they want to be together while in circle (e.g., respect all opinions, confidentiality, etc.) If it is an ongoing circle, the keeper might review the basic circle guidelines and invite the group to add more guidelines if necessary. Take a full round to be sure everyone has a chance to comment on the guidelines and to demonstrate their support of the final list. Remember that the guidelines are a living document and may be revised in circle at any time.

- Storytelling round—If the purpose for the circle involves a difficult issue, it may be useful to have a storytelling round. Invite participants to share a personal life experience related to the issue, perhaps in a very indirect way. Storytelling is a powerful way to move beyond masks and appearances to develop a better understanding of one another.
- Acknowledgment of those present—Remember to acknowledge those present in circle. It takes courage and commitment to participate in circle. Be sure to acknowledge the volunteers who have helped make the circle happen.

- Clarifying the purpose of circle—The keeper summarizes what has been experienced in phase one of the circle, using this summary to further set the tone of the circle and to clarify the purpose of the circle.

Phase Two—Deepening. Next, the circle may move into a deepening round of dialogue. This round gets to the heart of why the circle was called. Depending on why it was called, this round may include an expression of needs and interests in the case of a conflict circle, or the sharing of memories and grief in the case of a healing circle. If small group activities or sharing in pairs feels appropriate, it may be used here, but always come back to the circle and to sharing in the full circle.

Phase Three—Promoting Healing And Exploring Options. In this round, the focus expands from what's gone wrong or what's hurting to what can be done to make things right, to promote healing, or to initiate positive change. In many circles, such as those focused on healing, listening may be what's most needed—giving people a chance to tell their story and to have it received deeply. In other circles, though, exploring options helps break the sense of being stuck in either a painful experience or a self-destructive way of life.

Phase Four—Building Consensus Or A Sense Of Unity. Some circles, such as those involved in healing or understanding, do not require decision making. Instead, the keeper may attempt to create a sense of unity. Other circles do require decision making or resolution of conflict. In these circles, the keeper attempts to build consensus by building on each circle participant's input, weaving together the contributions of each participant.

Consensus involves an agreement among all participants to live with the outcome, to accept a decision or course of action because it promises the best for everyone given the circumstances. Generating consensus involves patience, creativity, candor about interest, and concerns and the willingness to think outside the box. We are challenged to set aside our personal agendas and fixed notions about outcomes so that something larger than any one person's preconceived ideas can emerge. Consensus is about dialogue, listening, and honesty.

To build consensus, the keeper may help participants identify areas of disagreement and give them serious consideration. The keeper can then use this fuller awareness of differences to work toward final decisions that are inclusive, and thus stronger.

Reaching decisions by consensus often takes more time than other decision-making models, such as voting. The strength of the process is that it assures that all participants will own and support the decision. When using this process, it is important that the group commit to addressing issues or concerns that may be raised on the way to achieving a consensus decision. One model for testing if consensus has been achieved is to use a consensus level system.

GENERATING CONSENSUS

Consensus is achieved when each participant chooses a consensus level of 4 or less. If any member chooses a level of 5 or 6, consensus is not achieved. If concerns cannot be addressed immediately, then create a process for addressing those concerns, perhaps at a future circle.

Consensus levels:

1. I can say an unqualified yes to the proposed decision. I am satisfied that the decision is an expression of the wisdom of the group.
2. I find the proposed decision perfectly acceptable.
3. I can live with the proposed decision; I'm not especially enthusiastic about it.
4. I do not fully agree with the decision and need to register my view about why. However, I do not choose to block the decision. I am willing to support the decision because I trust the wisdom of the group. *(Group finds a way to address remaining issues.)*
5. I do not agree with the proposed decision and feel the need to stand in the way of this decision being accepted. (Group finds a way to address remaining issues.)
6. I feel that we have no clear sense of unity in the group. We need to do more work before consensus can be reached. *(Group finds a way to address remaining issues.)*

Phase Five—Closing

All circles end with a closing ceremony that helps us to make the transition from the reflective circle space back to the outer world. Closings are designed to help us feel centered and to bring a sense of closure to the circle. They may include a poem, song or meditative music. Consider asking one of the participants, in advance, to offer the closing.

AFTER THE CIRCLE

Follow-up is one of the greatest challenges of the successful use of circles.

- If an agreement is made in the circle, it is important that someone follow-up to see if people are accountable to those agreements.
- If strong emotions are shared, there needs to be follow-up with the individuals to see how they are doing and ensure that they are getting the support they need.

TAPPING INTO COMMUNITY WISDOM: A GUIDE TO DEVELOPING AND MAINTAINING MUTUAL PARTNERSHIP
by Dale Nienow

It is empowering for a community to realize that it can solve its problems by tapping into its own wisdom. Community wisdom holds answers to even big problems; however, that kind of solution is likely to emerge only from within those communities that have taken the time to develop deep relationships that are respectful and reciprocal. The question is, "How do we make the shift to become that kind of community?" Methodologies like Gracious Space and circle are key approaches that can make a difference.

There are also specific strategies your group can employ that will move you in the direction of mutual partnership, and enable you to draw out the wisdom from various parts of your community. We offer these strategies in the first part of this guide; each of them requires intentional preparation.

The intention to cultivate collective leadership often starts with a group of community members who form a loose association and begin to clarify their work with each other or with an existing group that wants to transform the way it engages with the community. The suggestions offered here are to support these core leadership teams in shaping the initial approaches to tap into broader community wisdom.

Mutual partnership offers many rewards and some challenges. In the second part of this guide, you will find practical ideas for how to support the group's commitment to the collective leadership process.

SHIFTING TO MUTUAL PARTNERSHIP: FIVE STRATEGIES

It is common for diverse groups within a community to live parallel lives with limited interaction across groups. If you are interested in creating the mutual partnerships of collective leadership in which people actively share their wisdom and gifts, you must be prepared to invite some of those less-known people to join you in discovering a shared purpose—one that will lead to mutual well being. As discussed throughout this book, that requires taking time to open up and to be receptive to different perspectives and world views. This almost always results in being changed by them.

Here are some strategies for inviting people to open up and to connect in new ways. As you undertake this, it is helpful to realize that some of the work is looking inside at your own attitudes and behaviors. Some of the work is looking outwards with new eyes towards what is possible.

1. Pay attention to your own personal preparation.

It is important to spend time reflecting on your own feelings and beliefs about this notion of collective wisdom and its potential value to your community. Many people view leadership as setting bold visions or getting others to follow their direction. They may think of leaders primarily as bringing expertise or holding a position of authority. Those who want to pursue collective leadership can start by doing an honest self assessment.

- *How open am I to being influenced by others, particularly those from backgrounds that are different from mine?*
- *How willing am I to hold loosely whatever power I have in order to create space for partnership with diverse groups, knowing this means sharing power?*
- *Who are the people or groups who are challenging for me to engage?*
- *What do I need to let go of in order to open up to the wisdom of others?*

While this is an important initial reflection, we invite you to repeat it frequently as you engage your community more fully over time. You may find new and different answers as you expand your capacity to work from places of mutual interest and respect.

2. Name the compelling issue in your community that draws you and others, and then identify which individuals and groups care about this issue and have perspectives to share.

As you look for partners, it helps to look for the individuals in groups who are good bridge builders and who can model partnership. If you don't have much previous connection, it can be challenging to begin the relationship by starting at full speed in some joint action. Instead, consider using existing networks to learn about open community meetings and gatherings where you can show up and make connections with others who you believe share your common purpose. Typically, when you invite others to attend your gatherings, there is an expectation that you will participate in some way in theirs.

3. Invite conversations with bridge builders to elicit stories that open up to shared purpose and new relationships.

When you focus on discovering different gifts, perspectives and passions of others, you will build connection. Some questions that bring out what people care most about are:

- *When do you feel most connected to this community?*
- *What do you love about this community?*
- *What do we need to do to make this community healthy, just and inclusive?*
- *Who, if they worked together, could help this community advance?*
- *What goes on inside you when you experience or see someone experiencing injustice or exclusion?*

4. Collaborate with others to create venues in which participants feel they are on equal footing.

The dynamics of a meeting affect how power is distributed among the group. When you design gatherings, consider what gives people a sense of personal connection beyond positional or group identity. Even though people may be anxious to get to action and tasks, allocate sufficient time for relationships to develop. Provide opportunities for two-way exchange of views and information such as small group conversations. Consider some retreat gatherings to allow more opportunity for informal interaction.

At the Center for Ethical Leadership, we host two- to three-day Confluences in which we gather diverse members of the community around a compelling local issue. We create unusual linkages such as having a homeless participant room with a business leader. We invite people to learn from someone with a common passion and different life experience.

5. Sustain connections, understanding that we learn more through multiple exchanges.

Gathering the collective wisdom of the community is an ongoing effort. Relationships and dynamics that have been years or decades in the making do not shift in a single meeting. You will need multiple gatherings where trust can build and relationships can deepen. The exchange of wisdom and perspective grows over time. As you continue to meet, it will become clearer who is ready to be in partnership. One-time gatherings can increase awareness or provide information, but are limited in their ability to increase community capacity or to shift historic patterns of interaction.

MAINTAINING MUTUAL PARTNERSHIPS: THE CHALLENGE OF WORKING TOGETHER AS COLLECTIVE LEADERS

Tapping into community wisdom makes available a powerful community resource, but the accumulation of that wisdom is seldom tidy or orderly. And nurturing transformative relationships can make the process intense and time-consuming in the beginning.

Once the work is underway and many people are showing up to help with the work, a group undertaking collective leadership can get lost in all the moving parts. As long-time members leave and new ones come on board, the group can forget to pay attention to the patterns that help people bring their best to the work.

In addition, collective leadership relies on people taking ownership for the work rather than creating a traditional hierarchy to manage all the tasks that need performing. While that doesn't eliminate the need for people to take on roles to provide direction or to coordinate work, it does make for a much more fluid way of getting the work done. Collective leadership encourages people to identify what they can do to advance the common purpose while understanding what requires coordination with others.

Collective leadership also invites the group to stay open and to act on an emerging opportunity—even when that means reconsidering an earlier plan. While this way of working is very energizing and productive, it does require keeping an eye on the long-term shared purpose and on paying attention to how the work connects to what others are doing. Being open to learning as you do your work is also essential.

Here are ways to stay connected to the wisdom, passions, and gifts of community members.

Clarify roles and functions so everyone knows where to find out what else is going on and what else needs to be done.

Just because this is collective leadership and people are working together in different ways does not mean that you can forget the basic functions of project management and communications. What distinguishes collective leadership from other processes is that the people performing these functions are working to minimize their control and direction rather than trying to be the prime decision makers for others. As with all change processes, there are times when someone needs to step in and make a decision or set the direction—while checking to make sure that as many perspectives as possible are engaged before this happens.

Orient new participants to how collective leadership works.

The basic patterns of collective leadership—building deep relationships, crossing boundaries, trusting community wisdom, knowing your story and the one you want to create—involve new ways of interaction for most people. Having someone responsible for paying attention to how these patterns are practiced and for coaching newcomers matters. Eventually, as this becomes a way of life, everyone will be mindful of how they are carrying out their work and those joining will pick up these patterns naturally. However, in the beginning it helps to have someone take responsibility for the group's learning and practicing of these patterns.

Take time to step back and reflect on how it is all going.

Sometimes, you get so busy that you fail to notice that what you thought would happen isn't happening after all. Sometimes something happens that nobody expected and you would like it to happen again. Sometimes people feel good about what is happening, and sometimes people are frustrated or angry. At times, we need to step back and evaluate how it is all going. There are many ways to do this. Some groups have used storytelling as a way of looking back on what has happened. Some groups have an assigned staff person to check in with individuals and the group as a whole. Some groups hire an evaluator. Others find someone in the community willing to be a critical friend to their group, giving a look from the outside at what is going on and sharing that in an honest and respectful way. The point is to make time regularly for reflection so that you collectively assess what you want to continue, what you want to stop doing and what you would like to start doing to address concerns.

GUIDE TO HARVESTING AND SHARING STORIES
by Francisco Guajardo and Miguel Guajardo

When the school year begins, the first question we ask our students is, "What's your story?" Students are often bewildered by the question, but after several weeks of exploring the different components of a story, they grow more comfortable, more confident in sharing. The inquiry process is most critical in this enterprise. Teachers and others responsible for nurturing children and others as storytellers typically employ the use of questions in sensitive and strategic ways. Some of the questions we employ at the Llano Grande Center as part of the story production process are listed in the Anatomy of a Story chart (see chart next page).

As the anatomy metaphor outlined in Chapter 4 suggests, the navel of the story is tantamount to the core of the story, and the inquiry process helps us tease out the values in the story. The core of the message can be elusive, but through a questioning process, storytellers find their greatest

	ANATOMY OF STORY			
	Developmental Questions			
Parts of story	**Context**	**Main Idea of Story**	**What is the Action**	**Reflection on Story**
Navel: Core of message	Where does the story take place?	Who are the main actors and what is the purpose of the story?	What is the message?	What have we learned from this process? How does this story fit within the local history?
Heart: Values	What is the spirit of the place?	What do we want to reinforce as identity?	What core values do we want to share, instill or provoke to benefit the public good?	What are the core values we want to share, teach, espouse and practice? How will this impact community change?
Mind: Analysis	What will this story do to the place in which we live?	What are the (in)congruencies within the story?	How will this story inform, support, or disrupt stereotypes and myths in the community?	What are the (in)congruencies between the story and the community and its people?
Hands: Molding of identity	What is the story that will contribute to the identity of people and place?	How can this story celebrate the success of local people and place?	How will this story help people grow and change for the public good?	How have we developed/changed from this process?
Legs: Action of story	What skills do residents need that will contribute to the development of self and place? How can we put private stories to public use?	What are the highlights and points the story needs to emphasize? How will this act impact people in their development and as public people?	How can the story de-center/ disrupt the existing power structures to benefit the common good?	What is the impact of this action for future generations? Who benefits from this story? How can we imagine the future if this story is effective?

power when they determine the core meaning which resides in the heart of the story and use it as a guide to their story. The mind, or the critical analysis part of the story, is what helps us look at our stories through multiple dimensions by asking questions, at times by challenging certain assumptions that may have otherwise gone unquestioned. The hands of the story can hold and shape the identity of a community. Giving legs to a story is a very public enterprise; it's about telling the story publicly and finding if it has traction with audiences.

If you would like to have a more in-depth guide to storytelling, you can find a digital storytelling toolkit at http://captura.llanogrande.org.

JUST WRITE
by Lee Francis IV

Tonight
I am not a poet
I am a teacher and I have one assignment for you
before we leave here this evening
it's very simple
so pay attention

I want you

to write

that's it
no more
no less
just write

write a poem
write a story
write a novel
write a note
just write

write it long or short
neat or messy
upside down or backwards
just write

use pen or pencil
blood or ink
smoke or water
doesn't matter!

just write

I want you to write
the way you want to be held by your lover
in the middle of the night
write the steam of your first cup of coffee
the smoke of your first cigarette
the blood of your first heartbreak
nevermind the spelling
just write

I want you to write a playground
and the laughter of children
who aren't afraid of tomorrow
write a sunset
write a rainbow
write constellation
and then try this

I want you to write
a romance novel
about the first time you did the horizontal mambo
write a detective story
where the main character
searches for all the
weight
or socks
or people
you've lost over the years
write a cookbook
about the perfect way to make gingerbread houses
in the still cold winters of your childhood

and then
I want you to write
a letter to your
grandmother
the day she crosses over

write her all the things she's taught you
all the things she's meant to you

and then
write her face on the backs of your eyelids
write the feel of her hands
write the touch of her skin

just write

I want you to write in rhythm and rhyme
sound and body
your
whole
body
exploding in sentences
and paragraphs and
exclamation points

and a little uhhh
and a little more uhhh

I want you to write in bold tones
and saxophones and castanets
and electric guitar so raw
so powerful
it would make
Metallica look like
the Jonas Brothers

I want you to write
a tree
branches intertwining
with the sun
each leaf a poem
each bud a song
each song a story
of ancient times and endless days
spent basking in the radiant glow
of a thousand voices singing
I want you to write a journey to a far off land
where you don't know the language

but you understand the words

I want you to write a symphony
to end the suffering and heartache
of one hundred
one thousand
one billion people
spinning in place

write a Japan before the bombs
write a New Orleans before the storms
write a September before the ashes

write a world without hatred
or anger or violence or fear

and then write a day
a week
a month
a year
in the life of a child
a stranger
a lover
a friend

and then I want you to write your life
year heartsong
your past
your present
and your future
and that day when you can finally rest from your labors
that day when all things bright and beautiful
come to pass
and there are fireworks and glorious music

and your words
drift on the particles of light and dreams
in the brief brilliant moment

when all things are possible
because tonight
I am not a poet
or a writer
or anything else but a teacher
and I have one simple assignment for you

I want you to please

just

write

CONTRIBUTORS

ARTISTS

Delvis Cortes, "Building Community," artwork, Edcouch-Elsa, Texas
Reynaldo Garcia, "La Labor," acrylic on Masonite, La Villa, Texas
Dr. Shelly Valdez, artwork portraying traditional storyteller, Eastern Cibola County, New Mexico

PHOTOGRAPHERS

Elizabeth Bettenhausen, "Wisconsin collective leadership fellows"
Jim Blow, "Collective leadership fellows from Flathead Reservation"
John Guthrie, "Collective leadership fellows in Minneapolis, Minnesota"
Cheryl D. Fields, "Buffalo collective leadership fellows," "The Y.A.P Rap performance," "Elaine Salinas," "Olga Cardozo-Vasquez and Family," "Interlocking Arms"
Tony Lowe, "Sharing Our Gifts," "Saroeum Phoung teaches peacemaking circles," and "Mariah Friedlander and her mother, Anita Big Spring"
Dale Nienow, "LUPE Mural"
Juan Ozuna, "Friendship and art," "Story of early formation of selves: fieldwork in a different setting," "Discussion of story," and "Community Learning Exchange, Washington, D.C."
Eddie Rios, "Collective leadership fellows at Llano Grande Center, South Texas"
Randy Siner, "KLCC fellowship, Eastern Cibola County, New Mexico"
Isaac Singleton, "Liji Hanny and youth fellows from the Boys & Girls Club of Benton Harbor"

WRITERS

Ansel (AKA Hector Morales), "Friendship and Art," poem, Chelsea, Massachusetts

Shasta Cano, "Going Home," song, performed at a national coaches gathering, Lummi Reservation, Washington

Lee Francis IV, "How Story Began," based on a traditional tale and recorded for the Community Learning Exchange in New Mexico; "Just Write," poem, Eastern Cibola County, New Mexico

Mariah Friedlander, "Coming Together," Flathead Reservation, Montana

Harry Goldman, "Lonely Eyes," poem, Flathead Reservation, Montana

Sherry Timmermann Goodpaster, "Going the Distance," Northwestern Wisconsin

Liji Hanny, "Seeing the Gifts," "The Power of Intergenerational Partnerships," Benton Harbor, Michigan

Graham Hartley, Putting Community Wisdom into Action, an interview, Twin Cities, Minnesota

Misty Oldham, "Creating a Safe Space," Lummi Reservation, Washington

Saroeum Phoung, "You Can't Get to A Good Place in a Bad Way," Point One North, Chelsea, Massachusetts

Adam Roybal, "The Y.A.P. Rap," Denver, Colorado

Elaine Salinas, Putting Community Wisdom into Action, an interview, Twin Cities, Minnesota

Victor Jose Santana, "Know Your Rights—Find Your Power," Chelsea, Massachusetts

Eric Sotelo, "The Y.A.P. Rap," Denver, Colorado

Robert "Bob" Tenequer, "Seeds," poem, Eastern Cibola County, New Mexico

Marsha Timpson, "Take Me Home Country Roads," Caretta, West Virginia

Gayle de'Sousa Warner, "Moving from Judgment to Commitment," Tucson, Arizona

ABOUT THE EDITORIAL WEAVING TEAM

Karma Ruder

Karma Ruder is the director for community collaboration at the Center for Ethical Leadership (CEL). Over the past 30 years, she has worked in the public and nonprofit sectors to create processes that inspire people to move beyond differences and conflict into the creative territory of community and collaboration. She was part of the national coordinating organization for the Kellogg Leadership for Community Change (KLCC) initiative and served as the lead author for the *Collective Leadership Framework Workbook*. Presently,

Ms. Ruder leads CEL's work with local and regional change initiatives, and is involved in deepening and spreading the practice of Gracious Space regionally. Previously, she was the director of the City of Seattle's Neighborhood Planning Office, which engaged 30,000 citizens in creating their own plans for growing the city with grace. Those plans have since guided city investments of more than $500 million in Seattle neighborhoods. Ms. Ruder has a master's in public administration from the University of Kansas.

Dale Nienow

Dale Nienow is the executive director of the Center for Ethical Leadership, a nonprofit organization that helps people put values in action and to create environments where people work across divisive boundaries, tap into their potential and gifts, and bring forward their collective wisdom. He co-led the coordinating organization for the Kellogg Leadership for Community Change initiative and is co-founder of the Community Learning Exchange. Dr. Nienow serves on a variety of community boards and consults extensively with organizations and communities that want to advance social equity and implement more inclusive practices. He has a bachelor's in economics from St. Olaf College, a master's in college student development from Pacific Lutheran University, and a doctorate in education and administration from the University of Southern California.

Francisco Guajardo

Francisco Guajardo is an associate professor in the Department of Educational Leadership at the University of Texas-Pan American. Dr. Guajardo is also co-founder of the Llano Grande Center for Research and Development, a nonprofit educational organization based at Edcouch-Elsa High School in rural South Texas. His research interests include school and community leadership, Latino epistemologies, youth leadership, and family-centered instructional processes. He is involved in community leadership ventures, including chairing a citizen action committee that built the public will to pass a $112 million bond issue to construct new schools in rural South Texas. As an aficionado and practitioner of the arts, Dr. Guajardo joined other local arts advocates in founding an arts organization called Edinburg Dance Theatre. He holds a bachelor's in English, a master's in history and a doctorate in educational administration, all from the University of Texas at Austin; and an honorary doctorate of humane letters from Lewis and Clark College.

Miguel A. Guajardo

Miguel A. Guajardo is an associate professor in the Education and Community Leadership Program at Texas State University-San Marcos and co-founder of the Llano Grande Center for Research and Development. Dr. Guajardo's work has been informed by the local ecology and the values of fairness, good work, and democracy. His research interests include issues of community building, community youth development, organic leadership development, race and ethnicity, and organizational change. He is a fellow with the Kellogg International Leadership Program and the Salzburg Seminar and is a coach and evaluator for the South Texas KLCC initiative. Dr. Guajardo earned a doctorate in educational leadership with an emphasis on the politics and policy of education from the University of Texas at Austin.

Cheryl D. Fields

Cheryl D. Fields is a strategic communication consultant and journalist who is committed to social and economic justice. As the executive vice president of Langhum Mitchell Communications, she works with nonprofit organizations, postsecondary institutions, and foundations to advance their strategic goals with effective communication. Her work with the Kellogg Leadership for Community Change initiative helped to promote the practice of collective leadership and to position the Kellogg Foundation as a leading proponent in the field. It also led her to join the national planning team for the Community Learning Exchange in which capacity she produces and hosts a weekly podcast on collective leadership. Ms. Fields is a former fellow of the Poynter Institute for Media Studies, and holds a master's in journalism from the University of California and a bachelor's from Bryn Mawr College. She also is a dance instructor and choreographer.